"Crowdfunding is an essential skill filmmakers n... a complicated topic simple. It's a 'must-have' title I have added to my library. So should you."

— Elliot Grove, Founder: Raindance Film Festival, British Independent Film Awards

"Reading *Crowdfunding for Filmmakers* made me want to work at Indiegogo. In this second edition, John continues to blow me away with his ability to break down something as complex as crowdfunding into simple lessons that any filmmaker will find inspiring and immensely valuable. This edition represents the most cutting-edge best practices for crowdfunding creative projects."

— Rachel Allen, Campaign Strategy Manager, Indiegogo

"*Crowdfunding for Filmmakers* is one of the best resources for anyone trying to make a movie. I have lectured and taught at various public and academic institutions on crowdfunding, including Parsons and the International Center of Photography, and his book is the foundation of the fundamentals I impart to my students. The second edition contains very pertinent information on the evolution of social media and how to leverage those platforms. The specific examples Trigonis presents in his book provides us with the confidence to implement his advice. In short, I recommend his book without any reservations."

— Daphne Chan, Photographer, Filmmaker, and Social Media Strategist

"The Tao Master of crowdfunding for filmmakers is John T. Trigonis! In the second edition of his wildly popular book, he shares with you more secrets on how to succeed at raising financing using the tools of *Crowdfunding for Filmmakers*. This is a must-have for any emerging or established filmmaker looking to embark on the DIY, indie film journey and achieve success. I know I will have it on my bookshelf and encourage students and other producers alike to do the same."

— Rona Edwards, Film/TV producer; Co-author of *The Complete Filmmakers Guide to Film Festivals* and *I Liked It, Didn't Love It: Screenplay Development from the Inside Out*

"*Crowdfunding for Filmmakers* has become the bible of crowdfunding books that I recommend to (and even purchase for) people I know who want to run a campaign. It's the free gift that I give to some of my crowdfunding clients, and is the book I have on the table in front of me whenever I give a talk on the topic. What John has put together in *Crowdfunding for Filmmakers* works not only on campaigns for films, but any crowdfunding campaign regardless of the platform, genre, or goal. When I need a bit of the Zen Master of Crowdfunding's sage advice, I will lay to rest my old dog-eared first edition and revel in the expanded knowledge he's put together in this new book."

— Michael C. Dougherty, Crowdfunding Consultant and Film/Trouble Maker

"In today's modern landscape of filmmaking many folks use crowdfunding to finance their movies. Most campaigns fail because the filmmakers ask for money without presenting any real value for their supporters. Sorry, but this doesn't cut it. You need to have a plan and a focused direction if you want to experience success in your fund drive. How can you and your community of supporters both benefit in this relationship? The book in your hands is an instruction manual that will answer that question. You'll learn how to assemble a successful crowdfunding campaign that will put a smile on your face, make your investors happy, and get your movie done."

> — Forris Day Jr., Host of *Rolling Tape* podcast; Commentator for *Hitch 20* podcast; Reviewer for *antixpress.com*

"What do you get when you combine the ancient wisdom of Tao and the sage advice of crowdfunding mastermind John T. Trigonis? The second edition of *Crowdfunding for Filmmakers*. The first version became the go-to guide for creatives looking to raise money for their projects, and this latest one continues in that vein, updated for the newest realities."

> — Tari Akpodiete, Freelance Journalist and Documentary Filmmaker

"Crowdfunding an independent film is a lot different from what it was just a few years ago. The second edition of *Crowdfunding for Filmmakers* insightfully addresses how the medium has changed, offering invaluable wisdom on how to make your crowdfunding campaign a success in today's market. John T. Trigonis has lived through the evolution of crowdfunding, having worked on hundreds of crowdfunding campaigns at Indiegogo. He truly is one of the most important voices in crowdfunding today."

> — Essi Suomela, CEO and Cofounder, Spaceboy

CROWD FUNDING

FOR FILMMAKERS

THE WAY TO A SUCCESSFUL FILM CAMPAIGN

2ND EDITION

. . .

JOHN T. TRIGONIS

MICHAEL WIESE PRODUCTIONS

Published by Michael Wiese Productions
12400 Ventura Blvd. #1111
Studio City, CA 91604
tel. 818.379.8799
fax 818.986.3408
mw@mwp.com
www.mwp.com

Cover design: Johnny Ink www.johnnyink.com
Copyeditor: Gary Sunshine

Printed by McNaughton & Gunn, Inc., Saline, Michigan
Manufactured in the United States of America

Library of Congress Cataloging-in-Publication Data

Trigonis, John T.
 Crowdfunding for filmmakers : the way to a successful film campaign
2nd ed/ John T. Trigonis.
     p. cm.
 Includes bibliographical references and index.
 ISBN 978-1-61593-244-3
 1. Motion pictures--Production and direction--United States. 2. Motion picture industry--United States--Finance. 3. Investments--Technological innovations--United States. I. Title.
 PN1995.9.P7T85 2013
 791.4302'33092--dc23
                                        2012027342

for Marinell

...

the meaning behind my every line

CONTENTS

PART 5
THE *TAO* OF SOCIAL MEDIA

PART 6
ADVANCED CROWDFUNDING

ACKNOWLEDGMENTS

OVER THE YEARS I've met many talented filmmakers who not only make quality films and demonstrate an unbridled passion for the medium of the movies, but who have kept a keen eye on the future of filmmaking and film financing, and upon whose crowdfunding successes *Crowdfunding for Filmmakers* is based. To each of you — many of whom are mentioned numerous times throughout this book — I offer my deepest appreciation for your drive, innovation, and commitment to the art, craft, and business of making movies. Further thanks to Julie Keck and Jessica King, Gary King, Brendon Fogle, and Amy Jo Johnson for being tremendously helpful in offering greater insight into each of their crowdfunding campaigns. I would also like to thank Indiegogo's Slava Rubin and Danae Ringelmann for their encouragement and unrivaled dedication to crowdfunding excellence and innovation.

An extra special thank-you goes to my wonderful fiancée, Marinell Montales, whose encouragement initially pushed me to write the proposal for this book, which might have remained in my head indefinitely had it not been for her ardent belief I am the right person to literally "write the book" on crowdfunding for filmmakers.

I would also like to thank my good friend, colleague, and mentor Dr. James F. Broderick for his sage advice and helping me navigate the brave new world of publishing. To Alain Aguilar, Raul Garcia, Dani Shanberg, and Joe Whelski, best friends and partners in my diverse journey to create the next great work of imagination and wonder. And a special thanks to my family and especially the backers of my short film *Cerise*. Without their support, the mere thought of writing this book would never have crossed my mind.

Lastly, and with most gratitude, I would like to give a heartfelt thank-you to Gary Sunshine for helping form a more complete harmony between my paragraphs and my ideas, and especially to Michael Wiese and Ken Lee at Michael Wiese Productions for making *Crowdfunding for Filmmakers* a reality.

FOREWORD

by Slava Rubin, Co-Founder, Indiegogo

FOR AS LONG as I can remember, movies have played an important part in my life. In fact, even to this day, when I'm flying at 30,000 feet to speak at various events and give keynotes, movies are what help me pass the travel time most pleasurably. My love of movies was one of the reasons why Danae Ringelmann, Eric Schell, and I decided to launch Indiegogo at the Sundance Film Festival in 2008, introducing the ideas of crowdfunding and democratizing fund-raising to the world, starting with independent filmmakers first.

Getting a film financed is no simple task. For every one block-buster, there are hundreds if not thousands of independent movies, TV pilots, and web series that go unproduced because of studio executives whose job it is to green-light movies that are guaran-teed money makers, which is fine for them. But we believe that every movie should have a chance to be produced and distributed to the widest possible audience, including films that might not get a studio executive's thumbs-up. In the eight years Indiegogo's been around, we've seen thousands of independent films get made and thrive that might otherwise never have been given the chance, like the 2014 Sundance darlings *Dear White People* and *A Girl Walks Home Alone at Night*.

And movies like *Cerise*, the short film that propelled John T. Trigonis into the brave new world of crowdfunding only two years after Indiegogo's own launch. Although the campaign for *Cerise* was only seeking a modest raise, there were many elements that made it stand out from many of the other films being crowd-funded in 2010; from John's personal and charismatic pitch and the creativity in each of the perks being offered, to the promotional tactics he employed, it was apparent that he had ideas that not many other crowdfunding filmmakers at the time had, and he was able to execute them efficiently and run the kind of campaign that would be referenced for years to come.

After the *Cerise* campaign was complete, John did the only other thing he knew how to do, something that comes naturally to him, having been a university professor of creative writing and the humanities: He shared his newfound knowledge with other film-makers and content creators eager to learn the ways of the crowd, first as a series of blogs that earned him recognition on sites like Indiewire and The Wrap, and then as *the* book on the subject of crowdfunding for indie film.

There's no question that over the past two years *Crowdfunding for Filmmakers* has become a pivotal guidebook for first-time film-makers and even those who have one or two campaigns under their belts, conveying not only what works and what doesn't work in crowdfunding an independent film, but also addressing what kind of mindset filmmakers should adopt when preparing to crowdfund. As John frequently says, crowdfunding's a full-time job, and there are a lot of moving parts involved in making a campaign successful. Indiegogo does its part by providing filmmakers with the resources and tools necessary to collect funds securely and amplify a filmmaker's efforts to the widest possible audience, and John has done his part by giving them a manual that demonstrates how best to use those tools.

That's why in 2013 we decided to welcome him into the Indiegogo family. He was always giving freely his sage advice all across Twitter and other social media platforms, and we felt that if we could add someone with his unique set of skills to help our film campaigners create and run stronger campaigns, those film-makers would be able to build a larger awareness for their films and raise more funds so they could make the best possible film they can, with the crowd's help.

Since we made John our Head Film Campaign Strategist, he has mentored campaign owners and managers alike on how best to run a blockbuster film campaign, from *Super Troopers 2* and *Con Man* to other indie films like *Miles Ahead*, *Hardcore*, and *Iron Sky: The Coming Race*. Having spoken at numerous film festivals on behalf of Indiegogo and at TEDx, he has also positioned himself as a true thought leader in not only the space of crowdfunding for film, but on crowdfunding in general.

For thousands of filmmakers and other creators, *Crowdfunding for Filmmakers* has already proven to be *the* go-to guide on how to set up a film campaign for utmost success. *Crowdfunding for Filmmakers* 2.0 not only offers more of that evergreen advice, but also showcases more of the invaluable first-hand experience John has acquired over his three years with Indiegogo.

My advice? Turn the page and get reading! Our mission at Indiegogo is to get filmmakers, entrepreneurs, and other passionate individuals funding what matters most to them, and whether you're about to embark on your first low-budget horror movie or a documentary, web series, or sitcom pilot, John's advice is key to that success. *Crowdfunding for Filmmakers — 2nd Edition* has collected all his keys so you can unlock your campaign's highest potential when you're ready to bring your project to the crowd.

PREFACE

Welcome to the Future of Film Funding

Crowdfunding for Filmmakers: The Way to a Successful Film Campaign — 2nd Edition is a book geared toward the everyday dreamer who has always wanted to pick up a camera and make a movie. It's for the Do-It-Yourselfer who's used to saving up $500 and gathering a tribe of friends to shoot a YouTube video and who now wants to take video production to the next level. It's for the truly independent filmmaker who's made documentaries or narrative short and feature-length films through grants or investors and who now wants to stay on the cutting edge of not only filmmaking, but film financing as well. This book even goes far beyond the filmmaking front and can help visual artists, musicians, dancers, theater directors and playwrights, business startups, inventors, and many others raise the funds they need to bring their projects or products to the world.

But let's get back to filmmakers. Today, we don't have to be Hollywood studio executives to make films that look, sound, and feel like Hollywood blockbusters. The prime difference is money. The more we have, the more we can afford the talent and skills to make a masterpiece. Thankfully, the age of *crowdfunding* is upon us — reaching out to the crowd for the funds we need to make the movies we want to make and they want to watch. That said, this book caters to that community of indie filmmakers and moviegoers who seeks alternatives to the traditional, and crowdfunding has since become the preferred alternative to submitting scripts to studios, writing grant proposals, or finding investors who may only be concerned with a return on their investment. Over the past three years since the first edition of this book was published, crowdfunding has leveled the playing field between each of these extremes. It allows the everyday Joe and Jane the opportunity to bring their scripts to screen while at the same time grow an audience for the finished film before the first shot is in the can.

And perhaps the best part is that you don't have to be a tech guru or marketing maven when it comes to crowdfunding. You don't have to have a degree in business, either, and you certainly won't get sued if you crowdfund (though you may want to check with your accountant when April rolls around so you can keep Uncle Sam at bay). What you do need is a deep-rooted passion for your film and an uncompromising drive to move it from first page to scrolling credits. In terms of technology, all you really need is an email address, a Facebook profile and page, and a Twitter account, since these are the main methods by which you will obtain your funding — through rigorous online interactions. Other than that, add in a pinch of personalization and keep this second edition of *Crowdfunding for Filmmakers* by your side, and you'll be on your way to cooking up a successful film campaign.

Because what *Crowdfunding for Filmmakers — 2nd Edition* will give you *is* that cutting edge. A lot has changed since the first edition hit the scene in 2013. Yesterday's biggest questions were how much should I try and raise? and how many team members should I have? Today, it's how much *more* can I raise after I hit my goal? and do I need to hire a campaign manager? Back then, Facebook and Twitter were the only social media platforms you needed. Now there's Instagram, Snapchat, and Periscope to think about. It's all here in this updated edition that's on top of all the trends and even hints at what's to come for the future of crowdfunding for indie film, along with two brand-new crowd studies to better prepare you for your own crowdfunding journey ahead!

INTRODUCTION

The What *of Crowdfunding?*

IT'S HARD WORK making a movie. It's even harder securing the funds necessary to make one, especially at the independent level. Due to advancements in digital technology, just about anyone can afford a camera, be it a DSLR or a smartphone, and shoot a movie. Most Do-It-Yourself filmmakers learn their moviemaking skills through experience, wearing many different hats throughout the production process. The same goes for me. I've produced, written, directed, and edited eight of my own short films. Seven of those eight have been financed using my own money. No rich aunts, no lucky lottery numbers, just little amounts of money set aside here and there and lots of patience. But for one of my shorts, I decided to try something a little different, giving myself yet another title — *crowdfunder.*

Crowdfunding has become one of the most popular alternatives to conventional methods of film financing. It's a form of online fundraising, in which a person sets up a campaign, uploads a video, offers some rewards, and reaches out directly to the audience through email and social media. In February of 2010, I launched a crowdfunding campaign for my short film *Cerise.* During the campaign, my team and I raised a total of $6,300 — $1,300 over our initial goal of $5,000 — by reaching out to the public through email, Facebook, and Twitter, as well as by using the many tools afforded us by our crowdfunding platform of choice, Indiegogo.

A few months after my success crowdfunding *Cerise*, I wrote a trio of very popular blog posts under the umbrella of "The Tao of Crowdfunding." My first post, "Three Ps for a Successful Film Campaign," received an inspiring write-up on Indiewire, which helped it garner 1,600 views in only one month. It's now up to over 20,000 views and counting. "A Practical Guide to Crowdfunder Etiquette," my second post, did equally well, but it was my third post, "Twitter Tips for Crowdfunders," which was featured on independent film producer Ted Hope's Indiewire blog Hope for Film, that made me realize I had the kind of practical knowledge about crowdfunding that could help point other filmmakers and content creators toward the kind of success I had with *Cerise*.

Why "the Tao" of crowdfunding? Taoism is an ancient Chinese philosophy developed by Lao Tzu. In his immortal work the *Tao Te Ching*, the "venerable master" expounds on the importance of always keeping the universe and oneself in proper balance, of going with the flow and not challenging it, and of embracing simplicity and gentleness above all else. In the *Tao Te Ching*, comprised of eighty-one short verses, Lao Tzu also reveals to his readers the main tenets of Taoism: *Tao* (the Way), *Te* (Integrity), *Pu* (the Uncarved Block), and the principle of *wu wei* (non-action).

So how does Taoism relate to crowdfunding? Through my first-hand experience as a crowdfunder, as well as my years as a private consultant and most recently as Indiegogo's Head Film Campaign Strategist, I've found that when a campaigner remains true to the basics elements of fundraising — invitation, incentives, and interactions — the chances of achieving *over* one's initial crowdfunding goal increase significantly. Therefore, *Crowdfunding for Filmmakers: The Way to a Successful Film Campaign — 2nd Edition* centers itself around the offering of practical guidance, tips, and tactics about how to launch and maintain a lucrative film campaign simply by going with the flow of traditional fundraising practices and augmenting them with an added personal touch. The book examines various ways to meet and exceed one's crowdfunding goal through chapters that home in on team building, crowdfunder etiquette, and audience outreach through social media and other means of online interaction. You'll also find chapters containing "crowd studies" from a bunch of successful campaigns.

With lots of sound advice, examples, and the occasional tidbit of sage insight from Taoist teacher Lao Tzu, *Crowdfunding for Filmmakers — 2nd Edition* will prove as enjoyable as it is informative and fully acclimate you to the ever-evolving world of crowdfunding for independent film.

PART 1

FILM FINANCING

A BRIEF HISTORY

Chapter One

THE TRADITIONAL HOLLYWOOD MODEL OF FILM FINANCING

MAKING MOVIES IS serious business.

The bulk of all that I know about Hollywood and how motion pictures are made comes from the silver screen. In classics like Billy Wilder's *Sunset Boulevard* and Nicholas Ray's *In a Lonely Place*, audiences are given a romanticized glimpse into the hustle-and-bustle, deadline-driven lifestyles of screenwriters. Preston Sturges' *Sullivan's Travels* takes the audience through an intense ride as a drama director who has struck a losing streak tries to regain his mojo and ultimately discovers an appreciation for comedy. And in *The Barefoot Contessa*, Humphrey Bogart and company take us on a tour of how directors, producers, and casting agents go about discovering new talent and casting movies.

What these classics don't show the general public is *how* these movies actually get made financially. That's the part that makes the movies such serious business. Blockbusters like *The Avengers: Age of Ultron* and *Star Wars: The Force Awakens* aren't made with pocket change. It takes a lot of funds for Hollywood to put out the movies that it does. These movies are made by big studios like Paramount, MGM, and Warner Bros. using big money in the hopes of making that money back and earning a profit on this investment once the film is released theatrically to the public.

Today, the average movie can cost anywhere from $50 million to upward of $250 million. That's a far cry from back in the 1930s when a studio could produce a Hollywood picture for under $14 million. The 1939 classic *Gone with the Wind*, for instance, was made for between $3.9 and $4.25 million, according to Sheldon Hall and Stephen Neale's book *Epics, Spectacles, and Blockbusters: A Hollywood History*. Cecil B. DeMille's classic *The Ten Commandments*, with its amazing special effects for the time, was made for $13.5 million, according to Tony Shaw's book *Hollywood's Cold War*.

Today, Hollywood produces motion-picture spectacles laden with computer generation and top billing, all at costs that tip over into the hundreds of millions. The first *Superman* film starring Christopher Reeve was made for around $55 million in 1978; twenty-eight years later *Superman Returns* was made for $209 million. Seven years after that, Zack Snyder made *Man of Steel* for $250 million. At one time, costs were limited to lights, camera, film stock, the acquisition of rights if the film was an adaptation, and above-the-line expenses covering the director, writer, and actors. Studios still have to manage these costs nowadays, plus the costs of visual effects artists for films like *Pirates of the Caribbean*, which have budgets that can soar to near $300 million per picture. And these numbers just reflect the cost of production and do not include the costs of distribution, marketing, and promotion.

Again, making movies is serious business, and it's this kind of seriousness that has afforded the Hollywood studio system a powerful monopoly over not only the movie industry in the United States, but also the international entertainment industry. While I was at the Cannes Film Festival in 2011, I was stunned to see Johnny Depp's latest $250 million pirate escapade headlining alongside more artistic and less expensive films like *The Artist* ($12 million), which won the Academy Award for Best Picture that year, and *Midnight in Paris* ($17 million), a major contender for the same Oscar.

The independent film industry arose because of pioneers like Edward Burns, whose first film, *The Brothers McMullen,* cost an estimated $28,000 to shoot and launched an impressive and forward-thinking career for the New York native. But *The Brothers*

McMullen was not the first independently produced film; arguably, *Star Wars* was produced in traditional indie fashion, meaning there was no studio backing for the film. This, of course, was before the term "independent" or "indie" went from simply meaning an alternative method of producing films to becoming its own genre. After a slew of successful independently produced films had broken standard Hollywood tradition, studios like Sony, Fox, and NBCUniversal decided to subtly conquer this neutral territory by creating indie film companies like Sony Pictures Classics, Fox Searchlight, and Focus Features, respectively. After that, "independent" wasn't so indie anymore.

Thinking back to the days of *Sunset Boulevard* and *Sullivan's Travels*, it seems that if one wanted to be a screenwriter, a director, or even an actor, he or she would have to pick up and leave town for the neon lights of Los Angeles to nurture that dream into a reality. Flash forward to now, to a time when the all-powerful camera companies like Panasonic and Canon looked out and saw thousands of people all over the world who wanted to make movies, but because of Hollywood's iron fist on the entertainment industry, with all its beauties of fame and fortune, as well as its beasts of nepotism and cronyism, those dreamers didn't stand a chance at slipping a foot in the door. These camera companies ushered into the world the Dawn of the Digital Camera, and by doing so, gave rise to a new breed of *truly* independent filmmakers who all shouted in unison "Let there be lights! Camera! Independence!"

Chapter Two

• • •

THE DIY REVOLUTION

INDEPENDENCE, TOO, COMES with its own set of costs. The fact is that not a lot of everyday Janes and Joes can wake up one morning and say "I want to make a film" and actually do it without having set aside a substantial amount of money for the endeavor. Ever since the independent movement emerged from the trenches of World War II, ordinary people have been able to buy inexpensive portable cameras, shoot footage, and splice it together into a film. But even the people whom filmmakers tend to immortalize as the founding fathers of indie film — Dennis Hopper (*Easy Rider*), Francis Ford Coppola (*Apocalypse Now*), and George Lucas (*THX 1138* and, of course, *Star Wars*) — had already established names in the industry. So what about all the nameless filmmakers out there, the ones who have no connections, no desire to leave their lives behind for the star-paved promenade of Hollywood Boulevard? How do these filmmakers grab hold of a chance at possibly being the next Stanley Kubrick or Kevin Smith?

The term "independent" has gone through a metamorphosis and no longer means independent. It's natural, after all; a stock boy doesn't continue stocking shelves after he's been promoted to general manager. Even the prestigious Sundance Film Festival, which once served as a haven for indie filmmakers, has itself become a celebrity stalking ground, attracting studio films and those made by well-known indie personalities, as well as the occasional film from that neighborhood dreamer who shot his or her first movie on a smartphone and ponied up the $60 submission fee.

Now, this new incarnation of indie filmmakers, once only dreamers, has been granted the tools necessary to make their own films with newfound ease. Filmmakers like my best friend, Alain Aguilar, who dared to dream of one day making motion pictures. He didn't have to dream very long. The year he decided to pursue filmmaking was the same year Canon unveiled its XL-1 Mini-DV camcorder. Alain saved up $2,500 to buy the camera and make his first film, *Cog*. We shot the movie, edited it, added music, and eventually got it screened at NewFilmmakers NY.

But having a consumer-grade digital camera doesn't turn someone into an indie filmmaker overnight, especially if one's film costs nothing to produce. How can anyone make a film with no money? Easy: Make it with friends, something that just about every beginning filmmaker does. No one was paid on the set of *Cog*, either in front of the camera or behind it. I not only wrote the film, but I also starred as the main character. The location was Alain's workplace on the weekend; the food was leftovers in the fridge that his coworkers hadn't eaten; Alain edited the film using Adobe Premiere, which his company owned; and the music was public domain — if Beethoven's Ninth Symphony was good enough for Kubrick, it'd be good enough for us.

This was not independent filmmaking in any way. Yes, we were just as independent from the Hollywood studio system and their $250 million budgets as Edward Burns and Jim Jarmusch were, but without even the slightest amount of money to qualify as "independent," we couldn't really classify ourselves as indie filmmakers. A typical independent film budget runs around $500,000 to $1 million. Most filmmakers like Alain and myself don't have access to that kind of cash to invest in a movie. Filmmakers like us do it run-and-gun, guerilla-style, or what has become more commonly referred to as Do-It-Yourself (DIY) or as I like to call it, truly independent.

DIY filmmakers have an advantage today that they didn't have back in the late 1990s or early 2000s. A camera is the most essential piece of equipment one needs to make a film, and today filmmakers can acquire most top-notch cameras at very reasonable costs. The XL-1 was the height of 3CCD technology when Alain and I used it to film *Cog*. When I shot my short film *Perfekt* in 2005, we used Panasonic's HVX200, which was one of the first prosumer grade high-definition cameras on the market and was revered because of its ability to save files directly onto Panasonic's patented P2 cards instead of mini-DV tapes. Now, aside from Red and 3-D camera technology, many films are shot using digital SLRs like the Canon 7D, available for a mere $1,500, its younger brother the T3i, a steal at slightly under $1,000, and the 5D Mark III for around $3,000.

If an aspiring filmmaker really can't afford those amounts, he or she can always shoot a decent short film or feature-length movie using an iPhone or other mobile device that captures HD and 4K images; from there, it can easily be edited on iMovie for upload or export. In this sense, the DIY filmmaker has true independence. But good content — be it DIY, independent, or Hollywood — usually costs something to make, and that dollar amount doesn't stop at the price of a camera upgrade from a Droid to a Sony EX-3. For larger films, you'll need a larger crew since there are limitations to working with friends, especially if they are working for free pulling cables because they don't know much about how films are put together.

The need for money to make films doesn't stop at production funds. Later you may need editing or After Effects work done on your film that you yourself can't do. Or perhaps some CGI will need to be incorporated. Maybe the audio will need some adjustments. Sure, you can learn all of this yourself and implement these changes, but let's be honest — nothing spells "amateur" like seeing your name under almost every credit from "Writer/Director" to "Gaffer" and "Music by." Do-It-Yourself doesn't really mean that you literally do everything yourself; on the contrary, you do it yourself because you want to be the person with control over what the finished film will be, which means you're the person who casts, hires crew, and performs all the other producer tasks that will make your film a success or a forgotten dream.

That said, even the DIY filmmaker can't avoid having to find the funds necessary to make his or her film the best it can be. You can do what I've done for seven of my eight short films and wait a year or so working a day job and setting aside some of your savings for your $2,000 or $100,000 motion picture to happen. You can write up a few grant proposals and mail them off, then sit and wait for the boards and committees to decide whether to pay up or pass on your film idea. You can even try to find private-sector investors and hope they'll provide some substantial amounts, which will more than likely need to be paid back.

Or you can play it smart, be ahead of the times, and raise the funds you need for your film while at the same time build an audience for and awareness of your finished movie and keep full creative control. This way, you not only get funding for your film, but you also have a crowd that wants to see it because they helped make it happen.

Filmmaking, meet crowdfunding.

Chapter Three

CROWDFUNDING AND FILMMAKING: YIN MEETS ITS YANG

FILMMAKING HAS BEEN caught in a state of flux over the last fifteen years. The dawn of the digital camera has spawned a new breed of truly independent, DIY filmmaker rooted in the ideals of guerilla filmmaking. The advent of HD technology has given rise to a "Do-It-Yourself Revolution," granting these innovative movie-makers the same image quality and versatility that filmmakers like Denis Villeneuve, Ridley Scott, and even Steven Spielberg achieve in their bigger-budget films and blockbusters. So it's only natural to think that if these filmmakers were granted even the smallest fraction of a studio-sized budget, they might be able to create quality indie films at Hollywood caliber, but not at Hollywood costs.

Enter crowdfunding, a phenomenon that's been around since the 1990s, which serves as an alternative method of raising capital for creative projects. The concept is fairly simple: By launching a campaign on one of the many crowdfunding platforms like Indiegogo and Kickstarter, filmmakers can now go directly to the crowd for the funds they need to make their films, and with a few clicks on a mouse, mobile phone, or tablet, anyone can contribute money to those film campaigns with ease.

Currently, most crowdfunding is modeled after the "rewards-based system." Campaigns will include a video, which usually informs the crowd about the filmmaker and the nature of his or her particular film, and provides a list of rewards, or perks, offered to potential contributors in exchange for their money. The crowdfunding platforms serve as intermediaries that help out with this kind of online fundraising by offering important features like easy payment options and the integration of social media tools, making it simple for filmmakers and their supporters to share their film campaigns with their friends and other prospective contributors.

Despite reaching a critical mass of sorts in the late 2000s, the concept of crowdfunding can be traced back as far as the 1700s, its origins rooted in the earliest forms of microfinancing. The first time I ever heard about crowdfunding was when documentary filmmaker Gregory Bayne crowdfunded the money he needed to finish his feature-length documentary *Jens Pulver: Driven*. With a lot of hard work and constant social networking, he raised $27,210 on Kickstarter. This impressive victory made waves in the indie film community because Gregory was also able to generate such a staggering amount of funding (at the time) in less than one month from 410 backers — mostly fellow filmmakers and everyday people who had an interest in movies and mixed martial arts, the target audience for the film.

Since Gregory's triumph with *Jens Pulver: Driven*, thousands of other DIY filmmakers have followed in his footsteps. Some successfully funded films include:

- Phil Holbrook's feature-length thriller *Tilt* ($15,606 of $15,000 on Kickstarter)

- Brendon Fogle's short film *Sync* ($3,405 of $3,000 on Indiegogo)

- John Paul Rice's social issue feature *Mother's Red Dress* ($20,678 of $20,000 on Kickstarter)

- Sam Platizky's zombie comedy *Red Scare* ($7,645 of $7,500 on Indiegogo)

- Joke and Biagio's feature-length documentary *Dying to Do Letterman* ($55,140 of $37,000 on Kickstarter)

- Michael Ferrell's *Twenty Million People* ($13,515 of $10,000 on Indiegogo)
- Jocelyn Towne's feature-length film *I Am I* ($111,965 of $100,000 on Kickstarter)
- Timo Vuorensola's *Iron Sky: The Coming Race* ($636,000+ of $500,000 on Indiegogo)
- Laser Unicorn's *Kung Fury* ($630,019 of $200,000 on Kickstarter)

There is also auteur director Gary King's movie musical *How Do You Write a Joe Schermann Song*, which initially raised $31,101, then raised an additional $18,031 in a second campaign for finishing funds via Kickstarter. Filmmaker Jeanie Finlay ran multiple Indiegogo campaigns for her music documentaries *Sound It Out* and *Orion: The Man Who Would Be King*, raising nearly $60,000 through seven campaigns — a true testament to the power of crowdfunding as a serious alternative to traditional film financing.

Since all of these campaigns raised over their initial fundraising goals, it's easy to see that crowdfunding is not a passing fad, but a burgeoning revolution. In simpler, more Eastern terms, the yin of DIY filmmaking seems to have found its yang in crowdfunding. The yin yang, or *Taijitu*, is the primary symbol of the ancient Chinese philosophy of Taoism and represents the balance between opposing forces. In this case, those opposing forces are film-making and film funding. Neither of them can exist without the other. You can't make a top-quality film without some funding; at the same token, you can have all the money in the world, but if you lack the skills necessary to actually make a film, those dollars will be sadly misspent.

3.1. *The* Taijitu *is the Chinese symbol representing the concept of yin and yang, the balance and harmony in the universe.*

By carefully examining various campaigns over the years, as well as revisiting my own experiences crowdfunding *Cerise*, I've found that some people do it right, and others do not. Rather, they work harder, not smarter. I realized that most filmmakers don't consider themselves crowdfunders, never mind entrepreneurs, and therefore don't take time beforehand to research other campaign strategies like I had done and instead navigate this exciting landscape with a blindfold and a prayer. But this particular dream, in order to be realized, must always be seen with clarity throughout the duration of the journey we're about to begin.

• PART ONE •
SUMMARY POINTS

- During the Golden Age of Studio Films, Hollywood made big-budget films using its own in-house funds, shooting on the lot while hoping to clean up at the box office and recoup its initial investment, plus plenty of profit.

- In the Silver Age of Indie Film Financing, low-budget indie movies were financed using money from grants, private sector investors, the oftentimes difficult-to-secure distribution deal, and the filmmakers' own savings.

- The Crowdfunding Age of Do-It-Yourself Filmmaking is upon us, which makes it easier for everyday filmmakers to go to the crowd and seek the funding they need to make their truly independent films a reality.

• PART ONE •
EXERCISES

1. Think about some Hollywood blockbusters you've seen recently. Pick three of your favorites and research how much each one cost to produce. Then, do the same for three independent films

of your choice. Compare the quality, the content, and the cost of each.

2. Take a look at a few movies or web series on YouTube, Vimeo, or other online distribution platforms. How do they stack up in terms of quality, content, and especially cost, to the three indie films you chose in exercise one? How about your three Hollywood blockbusters?

3. Based on the above comparisons, start thinking about your own short or feature-length film, web series, or other video project. What kind of content do you want to put out into the world? What's the quality you want to achieve? How much might it cost you to achieve it?

**PART
2**

CROWD
FUNDING
BASICS

Chapter Four

Tao: Begin with the Basics of Fundraising

According to the *Tao Te Ching*, the word *Tao* (pronounced as Dao) means "the Way," and that way usually means going with the natural flow of the universe. So why might anyone want to deviate from that ideology in any other aspect of life, especially where raising money is concerned? The fact is that many of us choose the "the road less taken" to get to where we want to be in life, and that's fine, but only after you've taken care of the basics, which oftentimes do not change.

Certain elements of traditional fundraising should be implemented into one's crowdfunding campaign before getting into all the innovation and trial and error of this very contemporary technique. These aspects have been in place since the dawn of fundraising, and like nature, they are pretty much constant. They include essentials like building a strong team, deciding how much funding you need for your film, gearing your campaign toward a target audience, and forming and maintaining a campaign strategy. Without any of these elements clearly identified and fixed in place, you risk going against the natural ways of raising funds and will no doubt find yourself going against Scrooge McDuck's canny advice and working harder, not smarter.

Perhaps the only aspect that is new to the established model of fundraising is the idea of a crowdfunding intermediary through which a person runs his or her campaign. Fundraising has been around long before the age of the Internet, and so has crowdfunding, considering that one of the very first crowdfunded projects was the Statue of Liberty back in 1882, when Joseph Pulitzer turned to the American people to help raise the additional $150,000 to finish construction of the pedestal on which it would stand. So although the Internet was not part of the natural flow of fundraising back then, it has since become a vital part of crowdfunding today.

These next few chapters are all about going with the current that's been flowing strongly for hundreds of years so you can carefully plot out your film campaign and come out of it with few, if any, battle scars. The very first line of the *Tao Te Ching* boldly states, "The Tao that can be told is not the eternal Tao." Keep in mind that this is by far not the *only* way to run a successful crowdfunding campaign. It is simply the way that many indie filmmakers go about the process, the same way I went about it when I crowdfunded *Cerise*, and the same way I recommend you go about crowdfunding your film.

Chapter Five

· · ·

DECIDE IF CROWDFUNDING IS RIGHT FOR YOUR FILM

THE FIRST AND most important thing you must decide as a film-maker is whether crowdfunding is right for your particular film project. Other questions that will more than likely follow will be whether you have enough time to properly launch and effectively run a campaign for a month or two and if you have enough initial support for such an endeavor. For now, let's focus on one key aspect that most filmmakers don't realize is a pivotal starting point for making the decision to crowdfund a film project.

In order to launch a successful crowdfunding campaign, it helps to accept the fact that during the time you're raising funds for your film, you are temporarily no longer a filmmaker, but a *crowdfunder*. A crowdfunder, by definition, is someone fully focused on raising funds from the crowd for a project he or she will ultimately share with that crowd. In other words, if your script isn't finished, or if you're in the middle of preproduction, or if you're still coming up with a great idea to shoot, crowdfunding is probably not in your best interest at the moment.

The phrase that follows will be repeated many times throughout this book, and with good cause — it is an absolute, unwavering truth: *Crowdfunding is a full-time job.* Anyone who claims otherwise probably doesn't have a successful campaign under his or her belt. Therefore, whether crowdfunding is right for your film is partly dependent on your ability to temporarily minimize the Final Draft window on your screenplay, bookmark your *Cinematographer's Handbook*, and shift your full attention to fundraising. If you can do this, then we can take a deeper look at the question of whether your particular film should be crowdfunded, and that answer rests primarily with how much funding you actually need to make that film.

Something to keep in mind: As of this writing, there have only been a handful of film and video campaigns that have raised over $1 million, namely *Veronica Mars* on Kickstarter, and *Super Troopers 2* and *Con Man*, both funded with Indiegogo. There are plenty that have raised amounts in the hundreds of thousands of dollars, which is still a very impressive feat. But Hollywood films cannot be made on a shoestring budget; if your film calls for plenty of expensive computer graphics to tell its story, or requires locations that are difficult to secure, then crowdfunding may not be the best option for you.

Another reason most people may not opt for crowdfunding and instead start saving their own money or pursue more traditional approaches like submitting scripts to independent studios, writing grant proposals, and seeking the aid of private sector investors, is that they don't believe they have the support system to make a crowdfunding campaign successful. This, however, is a bit of resistance working its way into the mind. In truth, not many DIY filmmakers have the support of hundreds or thousands of people who might each contribute a dollar to a campaign, but that's where the idea of crowdfunding being a full-time job comes into play. You'll have to work hard to increase your initial support system. Its foundation will almost always be comprised of family and friends, because if they won't back you, who will? Then, once you start spreading the word through social media, you'll slowly but surely begin building a larger following and stronger fan base for your film.

It also helps to know that there are certain types of films that fare better in the crowdfunding circuit than others. Most documentaries, for instance, do extremely well, not only because they deal with real stories of real people, but also because many times documentarians can reach out to particular groups, organizations, and institutions for further support and contributions. Campaigns for narrative films may require more innovative and creative tactics to appeal to random people and get them to contribute. This is where a compelling story and unique incentives come into play.

Genre, too, can play a significant role in your crowdfunding efforts. By genre, I don't necessarily mean attaching the term "independent" to your campaign — the fact that you're crowdfunding is statement enough for its independence. Rather, is your film a horror film? Action/adventure? Romantic comedy? Some genres do better than others, but more important than genre is your *niche audience* — that very specific audience you're going to home in on most. Hollywood makes romantic comedies and sci-fi films (genres), but indie filmmakers make stoner comedies and social issue films (niches), which cater to very particular groups of people.

But before this, you will want to make certain there *is* an audience for your film, and the good news is that in today's world, there's an audience for every film. You simply have to tap into your niche and genre and focus your story, perks, and outreach heavily on them. Oftentimes, that also means targeting a specific demographic; for instance, if you narrow down your audience from horror movie fans, which may be a bit too vague, to Asian-American (demographic) hardcore (niche) horror (genre), you may be more likely to build a massive awareness of your film within the population most likely to buy into your film.

Another question to ask yourself is whether you can make your crowdfunding campaign relevant to your film's content. This is a question overlooked by many crowdfunders, but I find it's becoming extremely important. People like details, and it's human nature for us to look for patterns and connections in everything we see and experience. You should be able to tie your crowdfunding tactics directly or indirectly into your campaign. My short film *Cerise* is about a former spelling bee champion who's haunted by the word that took him down. The movie deals with words, so whenever possible, my campaign was centered around words, whether in the form of poetry-infused perks or spelling bees on Twitter. The more you can connect your film to your campaign, the more your contributors will keep your film on their minds, from its crowdfunding campaign to its film festival premiere.

Is there any truth to the statement that crowdfunding is right for certain projects but not for others? Yes and no. It all depends on your answers to the above questions, as well as whether you'll be able to nurture and sustain a desire in the audience to see your film once it's finished. This is very similar to marketing a finished film using a trailer. Once you watch the trailer for a movie like *The Suicide Squad*, the video has gone viral on YouTube by the next second, has been plastered all over Facebook and Twitter by your friends and followers within an hour, and by end of day, it's been reviewed by comic book and movie blogs across six continents. And why? Well, it's got Jared Leto playing the creepiest Joker ever, of course! But aside from that, a desire was created in people to want to see this film. With crowdfunding, your aim is to evoke a similar response in your contributors, but instead of a trailer, you have a more personal campaign video. Instead of the finished film, you have one that needs to be made, along with the passion and drive to make it. It's a challenge, but the tougher the challenge, the greater the reward.

Crowdfunding comes with its own set of challenges, which is why it helps to not look at it entirely through the eyes of a filmmaker, as it's far too easy to slip into the old-fashioned "starving artist" sentiment or declare that crowdfunding is not for you because you might be too proud or timid to "ask others for money." On the other hand, you shouldn't approach crowdfunding 100% like an entrepreneur either, as it's equally easy to fall into the chasm of the egocentric businessperson. The *Tao* of crowdfunding is about balance and harmony between these two seemingly opposing forces, making the process not about you, but about your contributors and, most importantly, your film.

Chapter Six

• • •

BUILD YOUR TEAM

How IMPORTANT IS having a team of like-minded people when you begin your crowdfunding campaign? A better question might be this: Can you make a film all by yourself? Sure you can; with a mobile phone or DSLR, you can make a perfectly fine short film that could be the next smash hit on YouTube, but no one will give you $25,000 to make it. Quality DIY filmmaking is a team sport. The only difference between DIY and Hollywood is money and manpower; Orson Welles said it best: "A writer needs a pen, an artist needs a brush, but a filmmaker needs an army." When a blockbuster like James Cameron's *Avatar* ends, the credits go on seemingly forever, and we as audience members see how many people it actually takes to put together a movie for our enjoyment. By contrast, when we see a film and every third credit names the same person, it verifies the fact that it was made on the cheap, which often translates to the film being of mediocre-to-poor quality.

To be taken more seriously as a filmmaker, eventually we learn that we have to start bringing people on board our films who know how to handle all the aspects of filmmaking that may not be our strongest suit. The same applies to crowdfunding. It's a full-time job to get from $0 to $20,000, and though you could do it alone, why would you? You'll be doing more work than you need to, which means you'll be going against the natural way and breaking a major tenet of Taoism, which we'll discuss in Chapter Twenty-Seven. Plus, part of your crowd will be composed of your own teammates, who will take on certain responsibilities while you focus on others.

According to data available through Indiegogo, campaigns that have four or more members on their team raise more funds than those being run by one person. The fact is that by showing there is more than just one member of your team, you build more credibility in the minds of potential contributors, making them think that this particular campaign may be more serious than another film campaign being run by a pair of high school kids. Crowdfunding is about community, and community starts with you and those closest to you. However modest it may be at first, there should be a team firmly in place so that others will take initiative and join your growing community.

Having a team is important, and in hindsight, I would've benefited greatly by having a somewhat larger team than my fiancée Marinell, best friend and *Cerise*'s cinematographer Alain, and composer Nino Rajacic. It's not enough to simply *have* a team of

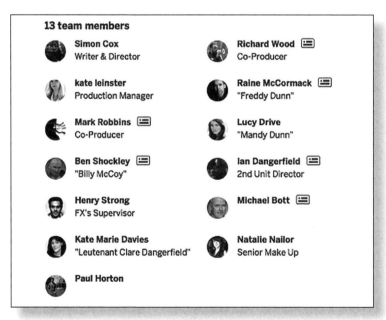

6.1. *From co-producers and actors to the FX supervisor,* Kaleidoscope Man *director Simon Cox makes sure to include the whole team.*

people listed on your film campaign; when possible, they should be the right people, those who each have "a particular set of skills" and who will prove an asset all along your campaign trail and help maximize its potential for success.

As far as your team is concerned — or *teams*, rather — I recommend having as many as three teams as part of your film campaign: your A-Team, in which you are Colonel "Hannibal" Smith leading a small band of skilled soldiers onto the frontlines; your B-Team, comprised of foot soldiers who can keep the work going through the hours and minutes of your campaign; and your C-Team ("C" for "crowd," of course), made up of allies and influencers from your crowd.

YOUR A-TEAM

Your A-Team should consist of the main people who are going to be pushing your campaign the most, giving their 110% with every tweet, status update, and email they drive out into the social stream. If phone calls need to be made, they'll be the ones making them. Meg Pinsonneault's A-Team of producer/publicist Lindsey Rowe and cinematographer Sabina Padilla promoted *Gwapa (Beautiful)* nonstop from the beginning of the project's Indiegogo. They didn't push hard only during its final days and hours. From day one they were on the frontlines for a project they unwaveringly believed in.

Again, my A-Team for *Cerise* was made up of Marinell, the campaign's primary marketing person, Alain, and myself. Alain not only helped spread the word through tweets and Facebook updates, but also wrote a couple of blog posts detailing what he and I were hoping to accomplish visually with *Cerise*, including some posts showcasing photos of our location scouts to get his network of camera-savvy cinematographers and photographers more excited about his next project.

YOUR B-TEAM

It's no secret that some aspects of crowdfunding are time-consuming and not very interesting. Or sometimes you're crowdfunding while at the same time trying to contact sponsors, influencers, and institutions to get them to donate something you would like to offer as a special incentive. Other times you may be trying to apply for grants, and filling out that paperwork can take time away from the more pressing matter of spreading the word about your film campaign.

Enter your B-Team, which I might suggest filling up with volunteers or interns. They can take care of some of the additional tasks involved with securing funding for your film. Volunteers are preferred because, in theory, they actually want to be a part of your campaign, and no matter how mundane you may think the duties you're assigning to them are, they will most likely be thankful to play any role whatsoever in the process of filmmaking. Plus, they'll be learning a lot about alternative methods of fundraising that they themselves might make use of for their own films.

Interns are like volunteers in that they might take part in your film project for the knowledge they will walk away with in exchange for their services during your campaign. You may want them to actively help with the crowdfunding, or you may want them to be the ones filling out the paperwork for various film and artist grants. This way, they'll learn how to fill out that paperwork and also grow accustomed to sending professional emails to organizations, which they may make use of in the future for their films. Furthermore, by doing this, they will leave your campaign with a network of contacts. Learning how to chat about your film with potential contributors might even give them the confidence they need to pitch their own ideas over the phone at a later date.

You may think finding an intern is difficult. As someone who has used interns in the past, I find it's a fairly simple process and you don't have to work at a university to be able to hire one. You simply have to go to the cooperative education representative at any college or university in your area and fill out some paperwork, which students will then peruse and, based on the information you supply, will choose whether they'd like to intern for you. Depending on the institution, you may be able to do it all online. And you don't have to pay the interns, since they will be given credit for the professional work experience, but you may want to treat them to lunch and offer a weekly stipend for their commute. It's that easy, and will make the processes of crowdfunding and simultaneously applying for grants a little less stressful.

YOUR C-TEAM

The C-Team, or Crowd-Team, is pulled together during your crowdfunding campaign and is comprised of people who, contributors or not, have become strong supporters of your film project. Many of these people may even be able to offer more than a contribution or series of retweets, both during and long after your campaign.

One example is the Indiegogo campaign for Charles Simons' web series *Deader Days*, a zombie comedy about a zombie named Daryl who's trying to fit in with the living. The campaign features actors' names along with a brief description of the characters they play (e.g., Jayce Basques, who plays Daryl, "your friendly neighborhood Zombie"), as well as crewmembers from writer/director down to the gaffer. But Charles, the executive producer, also got more creative and downright playful with the titles of his C-Team members who weren't a part of the production, but who supported *Deader Days* by writing blog posts, offering strategic advice, or, as was the case with me, tweeting very original messages about the film and campaign because of my job at the time as a freelance professor (hence the title "Doctor of Prosaic Rhythm").

The C-Team is anything but C-grade, and depending on how well you get to know the people whom you may be thinking of recruiting for your campaign, you may discover that they are very talented as well as humble and supportive. So don't be afraid to ask them to join your team. The larger the army, the wider the outreach, the closer you'll be to conquering your crowdfunding goal.

CELEBRITY TEAMMATES

If you are fortunate enough to have actors attached to your film who have some clout, be it in on social media or #IRL (In Real Life), get them on board the campaign helping to spread the word. Chances are they have a rather large following, which could potentially lead to some more contributions.

The concept of "celebrity" is an interesting one nowadays. There's really no such thing as a famous person *everyone* knows. But in the indie film community, there are plenty of filmmakers who've done wonderful things, who've won awards, and who would no doubt help a filmmaker with his or her crowdfunding efforts. If it's possible, those are the kinds of celebrities you may want to get hooked up with your project.

Keep in mind, however, that just because you have a "real" celebrity — like a well-known movie and television personality — on board your film campaign, you're not guaranteed an easy time crowdfunding your film. The Indiegogo for $12,000 in finishing funds for Sam Graydon's short film *Jenny*, starring film legend Gary Busey, brought in only 10% of its goal. *30 Rock* star Kevin Brown couldn't get the Indiegogo for a pilot episode of superhero spoof *Capes and Claims* soaring any further past the $460 of the $7,700 its campaigners hoped to raise, perhaps through Brown's notoriety alone.

On the higher end, we have Melissa Joan Hart's canceled Kickstarter for *Darci's Walk of Shame*, which couldn't get past $51,605 on an exorbitant $2M goal on the heels of Zach Braff's success with *Wish I Was Here*. Bruce Campbell's Kickstarter for his geek-geared game show *Last Fan Standing* didn't stand all that long after it got stuck at $20,550 on a $250,000 goal. And even James Franco, who ran an Indiegogo for his film *Palo Alto Stories*, based on his book of the same name, couldn't get past his impressive $325,929 on a $500,000. And this is James Franco!

Successful crowdfunding, basic or advanced, always takes a team effort. The more qualified your teammates, the more potential contributors you will have to win over, because every team member you bring into your campaign has his or her own following. If a person has a good eye for graphics and design, let him or her handle all of the design for the campaign, such as Facebook profile pictures and cover photos, newsletter designs, and poster art. If another person has a large filmmaker network on Twitter, let that person handle the social media for the campaign. And if you've got team members who have won film awards or those who are fortunate enough to have worked with slightly more famous names in the film industry, mention these accomplishments in your campaign, but do not harp on them, and you will most likely draw in more views for a look at your campaign video and a lift in your funds raised.

Chapter Seven

...

DECIDE HOW MUCH FUNDING YOU NEED

KEEPING WITH THE natural flow of the *Tao* of fundraising, after you've pieced together your initial team to help drive traffic to your film campaign, you should figure out exactly how much funding you'll need to bring your film from script to screen. This means doing some legwork and figuring out specifically what your film needs money for. The more accurate you can be, the better. Rough guestimates probably won't be enough; remember, you're asking random people to help fund your film, and people seldom part with their money without knowing the details.

Most people want to know exactly where their hard-earned money will go or what it will be used for. That's an everyday life thing, and crowdfunding is no exception, especially since there are more ordinary people out there contributing to indie film projects than there are Jerry Bruckheimers. You'll have to let your potential contributors know what their money will be spent on, so *you* need to know that information first.

BE UP FRONT WITH POTENTIAL CONTRIBUTORS

A general statement about what the funds you're raising will be used for should suffice for most people, so you don't have to get as detailed as a full-fledged budget breakdown, since most regular Joes and Janes won't read it. If you're raising funds for the production, it may not be the best thing to state that "the money will go to all aspects of the production." That's way too vague, and someone who may not know a thing about the filmmaking process could get deterred from contributing because you haven't offered any tangible information. If you state that the funds will go to pay the actors and crew and feed them, you'll be more likely to attract a contribution from a random person. If you're raising money for postproduction expenses like ADR or editing, mention that as well, because it's much more understandable to the average person than the word "postproduction."

I look at plenty of crowdfunding campaigns, and I see a lot of nebulous descriptions like this one for Sean King's Indiegogo campaign for his web series *The Gumshoe*: "$9,000 is need [*sic*] to produce the pilot, which includes four days of filming in Los Angeles, post-production and marketing." Words like "post-production" and "marketing" are way too imprecise for those of us who know little to nothing about either of them. Here are a few examples of campaigns that have explained what contributions to their film projects will be going toward. First, producer John Paul Rice keeps visitors to his Kickstarter page for his social-issue feature *Mother's Red Dress* from seeing red by bullet-pointing his funding needs. He starts out with a general note that "the funds raised will be used to complete the film now in post-production," but then delves into specifics, from hiring a sound mixer "who can deliver the quality of sound you hear when seeing a movie in theaters" to a visual effects artist who will "create all those incredible images seen in movies." He also includes examples and a link to a color correction demo on Vimeo so that people understand how important their contributions are.

Next, filmmaker Karen Pennington explains to the audience for her second Indiegogo for *Apocalypse Rock* that she needs "a little bit of moolah to pay for renting the RED Epic again and finishing construction of the miniature radio station" the last man rocking will spin discs in to keep himself from going insane during the end of the world. Karen also explains in a hearty paragraph that $3,000

7.1. *A rockin' example of a pie chart that's both well-designed and relevant for Shaun Colon's punk rock documentary* A Fat Wreck.

will go toward making the film sound awesome since "the movie is about music" and "it's going to have a lot of it."

This information should be kept all together and in one place in your film campaign's story so it's easier for potential contributors to locate, especially if you include an attention-grabbing header like "Where's the Cash Going" and "What's Coming Your Way" (*Ghost in the Gun*). Many campaigners are using well-designed pie charts to relay this information quickly and visually. Either way, the goal is to make your campaign information easily accessible so people will reach into their hearts and wallets more quickly, helping you and your film to the finish line.

WHAT IF I RAISE MORE MONEY THAN I ASKED FOR?

Back when I raised funds for *Cerise*, raising over one's goal wasn't all that common. Now, it's practically an everyday occurrence. In fact, in the "Advanced Crowdfunding" section of this edition, I'll be delving into "stretch goals" in Chapter Thirty-Seven. Most likely, you're raising the minimum amount of money you'll need to make the film you want to make, so if you get a little or a lot extra, you can do that much more with it for your film. I do suggest letting your contributors know what exactly you'll be doing with the additional funding, of course, since it is other people's money you're making your movie with, and they deserve to know what it's going to be spent on.

With *Cerise*, the goal was set at $5,000, and I ended up making it in a relatively short time. My team and I had extra time to raise more money, but I decided not to actively raise it because I had also saved $10,000 of my own for *Cerise*. "If more money comes in, then let it," I told my teammates. It certainly did come in — an additional $1,300 without my sending out a single tweet, status update, or email. As a result, I ended up coming in below budget and used that money saved to pay our production assistants a small stipend since they were all working for experience.

In DIY filmmaking, there's no such thing as too much funding, and there will always be something worthwhile to spend that additional money on.

Chapter Eight

• • •

CHOOSE YOUR PLATFORM

YOUR CROWDFUNDING PLATFORM is your campaign's starting point, much like the platform you stand on while waiting to catch a subway or train. It's your hub, your Grand Central Station, and every train you send out along the rails of the Internet — the Twitter Express, the Facebook Local — will ultimately direct your potential contributors back to that starting point. A crowdfunding platform is a website that aids in the fundraising process by offering crowdfunders a space to host their campaign and supplying them with the tools necessary to promote it to the world. Although there are crowds of these intermediaries ranging from forerunners like RocketHub to indie film–centric Seed & Spark, this book will focus its attention on Indiegogo and Kickstarter, still the two powerhouses that are synonymous with crowdfunding and are used by more filmmakers than any other platform.

A quick glimpse at Indiegogo and Kickstarter, as well as most other crowdfunding platforms, will reveal certain similarities. At the top of a campaign's homepage, you'll find the campaign title and a logline or other brief description of the project. Then there's the campaign, or pitch, video, through which you, the crowd-funder, will tell your crowd about your film. Next you'll find the perks or rewards, what your contributors get in exchange for their monetary support of your campaign. These elements make up the basics of crowdfunding, but aside from these constants, there are also important differences that you as a crowdfunder need to think about before choosing which platform is right for you and your film project.

ALL OR NOTHING VS. KEEP WHAT YOU RAISE

It is essential to keep a positive outlook and believe without a doubt that you will reach your crowdfunding goal. But even the firmest belief casts a subtle shadow: *What if I don't make it?* One of the most important things to consider when choosing a platform is whether by the end of it you want to walk away with some or no money in the event of an unsuccessful campaign, or what's known in the crowdfunding community as "All or Nothing" or "Keep What You Raise."

In the "All or Nothing" Kickstarter-preferred format, if you don't reach your goal by your set deadline, you don't get to keep any of the funds you spent all that time raising; so if your target is set at $15,000 for your feature-length comedy and you only raise $14,500, you get nothing for your efforts. In the "Keep What You Raise" or "Flexible" model popularized by Indiegogo, if you don't raise the entire $15,000 for your film and instead only raise $5,000 by your deadline, you get to keep the $5,000 you did earn.

There are pros and cons to each of these models. The "All or Nothing" variety may seem like too much of a risk, and many filmmakers, particularly those who may not have a strong enough fan base to guarantee a successful campaign, might shy away from this. Others view it in a very positive way, as it adds a certain sense of immediacy to a campaign, which makes people more inclined to contribute right away instead of waiting and perhaps hoping the crowdfunder makes his or her goal before they get the chance to type in their credit card numbers.

Something else to consider when choosing a platform is when the money is taken from the contributor and disbursed to the crowdfunder. When a backer clicks the "Contribute Now" button on Indiegogo, for instance, that contribution is taken out of his or her account or credit card immediately, whereas with Kickstarter, the backer's information is taken and held until there's a green banner streaming across the campaign that reads "Funding Successful," at which point all the contributors' credit cards are collectively swiped.

Choosing a platform is all about options, and as a crowdfunder, you have to figure out what will be best for your specific film campaign. If you're trying to make a sci-fi feature for $100,000 that requires stunts and shooting locations, chances are you might be more inclined to try your luck with Kickstarter, or go with Indiegogo and select its "Fixed" funding option, which is essentially "All or Nothing," since if you only end up raising $2,000, there's not a whole lot you'll be able to do with what amounts to 2% of your projected budget. However, if you're making a short film for $5,000 and raise only $3,500, you may still be able to put together a very decent short film, in which case Indiegogo would be the only choice.

TOOLS OF THE TRADE

As with anything else, the right tools can get the job done right and with fewer headaches. Therefore, another decisive factor when choosing a crowdfunding platform is finding out what tools each one has at its disposal to make the arduous task of raising funds a bit more bearable. Here are three of the basic tools that both Indiegogo and Kickstarter offer to their users, which are usually located at the top of your campaign page:

- Story/Campaign
- Updates
- Comments

"Story/Campaign" makes it easy to get visitors back to your main page on which your video, description, and incentives are located. "Updates" are how crowdfunders can keep contributors in the loop with what's going on with the campaign. Contributors can interact with the campaigners as "Comments." Indiegogo also offers a "Backers" tab, which lists the people who've contributed to your project. Here, contributors can control what information to keep private and what to publicize, such as the amount given, in the event a contributor wants to keep the exact amount he or she gave out of the spotlight, or his or her identity, in case someone wants to remain anonymous.

Another tool that Indiegogo offers that Kickstarter doesn't is its "Gallery," which appears as a tab once you upload images or embed videos directly to your campaign. I found the gallery extremely helpful during my campaign for *Cerise*. Here's an example of some of the things that Sam Platizky, writer, producer, and crowdfunder for *Red Scare*, a zombie farce of 1950s propaganda movies, included in his gallery:

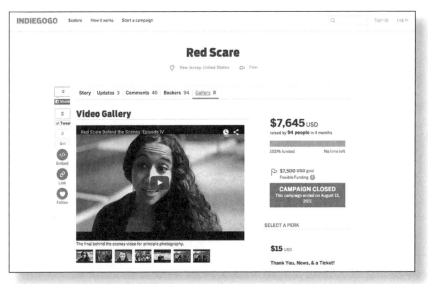

8.1. *The* Red Scare *team's gallery is filled with fun videos for potential contributors to peruse.*

Sam used his Indiegogo gallery primarily for posting video updates about the progress of *Red Scare* and also included the design he ultimately used for his T-shirts perk. Although the gallery has lost some of its functionality now that you can embed images and video directly into your Indiegogo campaign's story, it can be a very helpful addition to a rigorous campaign and can also serve as a time capsule of your days or weeks as a crowdfunder.

SOCIAL MEDIA INTEGRATION

All crowdfunding platforms have what usually proves to be the most important feature in any platform — social media integration. The difference between crowdfunding and traditional fundraising is the fact that if you're choosing a website to host your project, you'll probably be using the Internet as your primary method of bringing in funds, and today that means email and social media. Indiegogo and Kickstarter cover the basic social networking sites, namely Twitter and Facebook, and make it easy for you to share your project with your friends and the rest of the world.

Most crowdfunding platforms include a "Share" toolbar, which is typically located beneath or beside your campaign video, and which includes an "Embed" button and a trackable "shortlink" so you can see how many clicks you get on your link. This can prove highly important for recording metrics about your campaign, which can give you a sense of what may be working and what may not be, numerically speaking, of course.

ANALYTICS

Speaking of numbers, the ability to keep track of what's going on with your campaign behind the scenes can be a very important factor as well, and some crowdfunding platforms do it more effectively than others. In general, analytics tell you critical information about your film campaign, like how many views your campaign has gotten versus how many contributions, what websites are driving contributions, and from where in the world these funds raised are coming. Again, some platforms offer better analytics than others; Indiegogo's "Dashboard" shows how many of your funders have referred someone else to your Indiegogo page, and even lets you see how much money was brought in by a contributor's referral. For example, on my page, I know that I referred fourteen people, seven of whom became contributors giving a total of $335 to *Cerise*. Friend and fellow crowdfunder Gary King referred 161 people, and out of that three of them contributed an additional $235. Marinell referred an impressive 222 people, with one of them giving my short film $10.

These are some interesting metrics to keep track of, but keep in mind that they are only accurate if you're making use of the social networking widgets found in the "Share" toolbar of your campaign. I didn't make use of them, because in reality, I didn't just share my film to fourteen people; I did the bulk of my promotion directly through Facebook, Twitter, and my email. Again, this shows how important it is to make use of the tools your crowdfunding platform provides and learn how to use them to benefit your campaign efforts most.

CUSTOMER SERVICE

If you have any questions, you shouldn't hesitate to contact the company's customer support, especially if this is your first time crowdfunding. If customer support is an important feature to you, then Indiegogo will prove the better platform since it is renowned for its first-rate Customer Happiness Team, whereas Kickstarter lags far behind in this arena. In fact, when actor, writer, and filmmaker Gregor Collins finished crowdfunding for his feature-length dramedy *It's a Good Day to Die*, he was so disappointed with Kickstarter's lack of customer service skills that he wrote a letter called "Wake Up, Kickstarter," which appeared on the website Film Courage. In it, Gregor explains to the indie film community that Kickstarter doesn't care about its customers the way, say, Apple does. "At the end of our campaign," his P.S. begins, "we pay you

5% of our hard-fought-for money. So I don't think it's unreasonable to expect at least 5% effort on your part to be genuine."

Today, customer service can also fall into the realm of social networking, and your crowdfunding platform should have an active Twitter and Facebook account and should be doing more than simply promoting its "Project of the Day." If you have a quick question that can be answered in 140 characters, you should be able to ask it to @Indiegogo or @Kickstarter and receive a timely reply. That's what customer happiness is really all about — timeliness and efficiency.

Research Your Platform

These are the basics you need to consider before choosing the right platform for your crowdfunding campaign. You probably won't find a platform that has everything you're looking for, but if you can check off as many of these platform assets as you can, it will no doubt lead to a more productive and enjoyable crowdfunding experience. And you will also want to keep as up to date as possible with all that these two platforms are doing for the future of crowdfunding for filmmakers, from innovations like Indiegogo's InDemand, which allows successfully funded campaigns to "stay open" after their deadlines to continue raising funds, to "equity crowdfunding." (More on this in Chapter Thirty-Six.)

But no matter what platform you choose, many other factors need to be implemented and executed in order to get your campaign from zero to multiple zeros, and the question in your head should not be *What can this crowdfunding platform do for me?* but rather *What can I do with this particular crowdfunding platform?* That said, my biggest advice would be to do some extra research into the top three or five crowdfunding platforms for indie film — especially these two crowdfunding dynamos — and see which platform you can make the best use of with your time.

• • •

Chapter Nine

HOME IN ON YOUR TARGET AUDIENCE

IN TODAY'S WORLD, anybody who has a halfway decent idea, a modicum of skill with a camera, and a slight sensitivity to the art of storytelling can be a filmmaker. Most often, the film's success has less to do with the quality of the finished product than with the fact that the filmmakers took time to focus on their target audience. Lots of filmmakers settle for wanting to make a movie that everyone will enjoy. But who's *everyone?* With so many different tastes in films out in the world, we traditionally break those tastes up into single-word genres like action, comedy, drama, thriller, and western. But since the inception of these genres, the world has grown vaster, and as a result, those genres have been broken down into smaller categories that include psychological thrillers, bromances, and dramedies, so that we as filmmakers can reach out to even more people by targeting those particular audiences.

But it hasn't stopped there. Genres have been broken down into niches, very tightly focused audiences who enjoy certain elements that mainstream movies don't always address. It's all a microcosm within a macrocosm, and it is this smallest cosmos that today's filmmakers should aspire to and find success in on their way up the stairway to the stars. The same way you'll ultimately devise an idea that caters to a particular genre and niche, your crowdfunding campaign should home in on that very specific target audience as well.

That's the basic concept behind crowdfunding — you're not running a campaign solely to secure the funds you need to make your film, you're raising awareness from an audience that wants to see your film. You're building a fan base with every dollar added to your crowdfunding goal. Once your film is complete and ready to screen at film festivals or through online distribution, you'll have an army of people in various regions eagerly awaiting it because they not only enjoy films like yours, but they also helped fund your film.

That said, it's very important to figure out who your target audience is *before* you launch your campaign, and that takes a little research to see which niches and communities your film will be most relevant to. Sometimes, this is fairly easy. *Mother's Red Dress* is billed on its Kickstarter as "a social issue feature film," so of course now we have a better idea of the kinds of people who will watch it, namely, the socially conscious. But even with this very focused niche of "social issues," we have to try to dig even deeper and ask what kind of social issue does the film focus on. A brief read through the description reveals that *Mother's Red Dress* is about "abuse, domestic violence and mental illness," according to Kyra Dawson of the website The Scribe's Desk. But producer and campaigner John Paul Rice also delves deeper in one section of his Kickstarter that he titled "our motivation to tell this story," in which he states the following:

> A tragic love story, the film deals with the effects of domestic violence, abuse and mental illness. The message of the film is that the denial of trauma causes mental dysfunction. We created a film based on the hope that the main character would possibly begin his road to recovery once he faced the truth of his past.

It's very important to get as factored down to your true target audience as possible if you're going to have a smooth and successful campaign and film. Just like the simple phrase "social issue" adds much to this film's niche and genre, so does the phrase "hardcore horror" in the Kickstarter for *Hardcore Indie*, a documentary about the making of two hardcore horror films, *Crawl or Die* (then called *Crawl*), directed by Oklahoma Ward and starring Nicole Alonso, and *Screen*, directed by David Paul Baker. Sometimes a niche or two can be in the title of your film, as in *Ninjas vs Monsters*, directed by Justin Timpane, which will no doubt appeal to people who enjoy a good martial arts film as well as those who like monster movies.

The real work about homing in on your target audience is figuring out where to find that audience, and that means asking yourself two questions: *Who will watch my movie?* and *Who might help me promote my film and my crowdfunding campaign?* Luckily, the Internet makes both of these tasks a lot less intimidating, and with a few hours researching key word results on Google, you'll swiftly work your way from the outer rings to the bull's-eye.

WEBSITES AND BLOGS

Websites are probably the first place you should start to seek out your target audience and immerse yourself in that genre or niche. I subscribe to the belief that it's always best to start big and work your way down. So if I were making a zombie film, for instance, the first sites I'd sign up for or subscribe to would be biggies like Fangoria, Bloody Disgusting, and Rue Morgue. But a quick Google search of "zombie websites" reveals a slew of great undead resources, plus a "World's Best Zombie Sites" list from *www.toptenlist.com*, which contains sites ranging from zombie games and web content like the Code Z series to the *My Living Dead Girl* comic. As the list's tagline states, "Welcome to the Web of the Living Dead!"

Now, a refined search of "zombie movie websites" reveals a slew of online venues where you can watch zombie movies to your heart's content, and perhaps interact with other zombie movie fans. After all, if they like similar movies, chances are they might like yours, too. A further refined search of "zombie comedies" shows us a side-scrolling list of the most mentioned zombie movies on the Web, with *Shaun of the Dead*, *Zombieland*, and Sundance darling *Dead Snow* leading the charge. But the search also affords us the names of websites where we can start conversations with other like-minded zombie-lovers, as well as a "Ten Best Zombie Comedies of All Time" list, courtesy of Film Racket.

Ultimately, after working your way into this particular community by interacting with other zombie film fans on these websites, in forums, and on social media and sharing valuable content with your fellow *Walking Dead*sters, you can gradually start mentioning *your* zombie comedy. Eventually, you'll start building a following of people who will be excited to see your film, but more importantly, you may have a newfound network of people who'll help you with its funding and spreading the virus out further. Hence, your undead army begins to seed.

Blog sites are another powerful resource to help you zero in on your target audience. If you're making a bromance, you'll find tons of blogs maintained by people who enjoy a fun story about guys being guys like *The Hangover* and *Harold & Kumar Go to White Castle*. After searching "bromance," and after a bit of scrolling down from Wikipedia and Urban Dictionary definitions, you'll find a bunch of blogs, including a Tumblr called A Bromance Appreciation Blog, that will prove helpful at building a budding bromance between you and your audience.

FACEBOOK SEARCHES

Okay, back to zombies for a moment. A quick search on Facebook gives us a list of pages with the word "zombie" in it. Today, this includes well-known intellectual property at the top of the list — from apps like Zombie Island to TV shows like *iZombie*, and even Rob Zombie himself. (This would not have been the case years ago when the first edition of this book came out, but now that all fans' attention is on social media and mobile devices — what's commonly referred to as the "second-screen experience" — even the larger players have to compete in a world where good content is plentiful.) But if you keep scrolling down the search page, you'll begin to see pages for The Zombie Apocalypse Defense Force, which promotes all things undead and horror to a following of over 140,000 people; the Omaha Zombie Walk, with over 5,000 fans; and a slew of other, more independently owned Facebook pages for websites, as well as pages for fellow zombie fiction creators, be they other filmmakers, authors, musicians, or mobile game developers.

Click the "Like" button on a bunch of the pages you're genuinely intrigued by, and then start interacting with these pages. Then, by the time you launch your crowdfunding campaign, you may be initiated into these communities enough to be able to post a link to your campaign on the wall, for all those hardcore zombie fans out on that page to see; and out of, say, the 140,000 fans on the ZADF's Facebook page, there's no telling how many of them might actually contribute to your campaign or at least share it with their own Facebook friends. The potential here can be huge. It's just a matter of setting up a derrick and tapping into this fertile landscape and there's no doubt some funds will flow.

Again, it's imperative that you first spend time on any Facebook pages you click "Like" on and engage with some of the other fans posting on that page. "Like" the posts you like, but comment on them too. Social media is about being social, so get social and you'll find more people taking heed of you and your campaign once you've earned their attention.

TWITTER SEARCHES

Equally as important as Facebook, blog, and web searches in discovering and maximizing your target audience are Twitter searches.

You can discover an entire world of potential contributors and supporters for your crowdfunding campaign and build it up into a powerful audience. When I started raising funds for *Cerise*, I only had a couple hundred Twitter followers, and through the course of the campaign, that number doubled. Now, I have nearly 10,000 followers. When you indulge in conversations with the people you follow and participate in Tweetchats like #FilmCurious, Seed & Spark's weekly discussion about movies, crowdfunding, and distribution, or the very popular #Scriptchat, by the end of that hour or so of chatting, you'll usually end up with three to ten new followers each week.

Your main concern should be tapping into not only film-centric groups, but also those that relate to the genre and niches of your film. And again, it's important to begin this process long before you start crowdfunding to ensure that the people you meet know you're on Twitter for the right reasons, and not only because you need funding for your next indie film.

I often mention at seminars and panels the impressive fact that 70% of the funds I received during my Indiegogo for *Cerise* came from strangers, and people's eyebrows perk up immediately. I attribute this to the fact that I had started my outreach early on, even before I knew there was such a thing as crowdfunding. Because of this, *Cerise* became a featured project on Indiegogo fairly quickly, and as a result, I attracted the attention of many wonderful people like Ryan Ronning, Ben Gerber, and Gavin ap'Morrygan. By keeping up with your activity and showing that you are a crowdfunding force to be reckoned with, you'll be given more opportunities to demonstrate your drive and passion to the communities you've joined, and they will see that drive and passion, and you will be rewarded for it tenfold.

Chapter Ten

• • •

CREATE (AND MAINTAIN) YOUR CAMPAIGN STRATEGY

ONCE YOU'VE ESTABLISHED the target audience for your film as well as for your crowdfunding campaign — from the overall genre down to the most exact niche — it's time to figure out how to reach that audience. And once you reach the audience, the next and more important part becomes how to keep them engaged and checking in on your film's status long after its campaign has ended. The ultimate question, however, is how do you keep your film on people's minds without becoming a total nuisance?

It is therefore highly important to not dive into your crowdfunding campaign blindfolded. Too often, people go in with the attitude that they're just going to "try it out and see if it actually works," and yes, I was guilty of this too. The fact is that it does work: As of January 2016, Kickstarter helped to raise over $321 million in funding for its successful film and video projects since the platform began in 2009. In April 2012, President Obama signed into law the JOBS (Jumpstart Our Business Startups) Act, which makes equity investment possible through crowdfunding (read more about this in Chapter Thirty-Six). This development was preceded by the president joining forces with Indiegogo for his Startup America Partnership offering small businesses and entrepreneurs the chance to raise up to $30 million in startup capital.

Whether it'll work for you depends on whether you "do [it] or do not," because, as Jedi Master Yoda dictates, "there is no try." The worst-case scenario is that if you only "try it out" and fail, you've hopefully learned a lot from the experience, but it will be at the expense of having lost some credibility with the people who may have already funded you and your film, which means you'll have to spend your time searching for a whole new core of supporters and contributors for your next crowdfunding attempt. So, if you're going to crowdfund, do it for real, with the intention of taking home well over your initial fundraising goal. To do this, you need to have a strategy in mind.

When you watch TV commercials like the ones from Geico and Progressive, each commercial seems to build off of the next, and that's all part of the marketing strategy for these car insurance companies. Someone planned this out long before Geico launched the first of its "It's so easy, a caveman could do it" campaign. Similarly, your entire crowdfunding campaign, like any compelling story, should have a beginning, middle, and end. Traditionally in fundraising, this could be seen as the *launch, run,* and *fulfillment.* The forward direction of a film should be set up during the first act, its beginning, and so should your campaign, so that when you launch, it will start off strong and grab the attention of your target audience. It's the pivotal second act, however, that can make or break the film experience for its viewers, so the second act of your campaign should be soundly spliced together and unveil new and interesting things at every twist and turn. The majority of those twists and turns should be set up before the launch. By the end of a film, an audience wants fulfillment, so by the conclusion of your campaign, your contributors should feel just as fulfilled when they receive their incentives in a timely manner.

Much of your campaign's strategy should revolve around the central themes and concepts present in your film. While you *can* run a campaign in a more straightforward manner, offering standard incentives like executive and associate producer credit and T-shirts, it probably won't be much fun for you to run. More importantly, it may start to feel a bit flat to potential contributors. As crowdfunders, we should go the distance with our campaigns in the same way we would as filmmakers making our movies because people will undoubtedly see the effort that is poured into a campaign and appreciate it even more, which could mean the difference between receiving a $10 contribution and a $50 one.

When strategizing your campaign, think about the important themes and motifs that are running through it. Once you've got those elements identified, think about how you can bring them into the campaign experience. For instance, thematically, *Cerise* is a movie about how something from one's past can keep him or her from realizing his or her full potential. How did I work that concept into my crowdfunding campaign? Easy: I didn't. It's too grandiose an idea, not to mention very abstract. But *Cerise* also revolves around the fact that the protagonist is a spelling bee champ who lost because of a single word. So, I took the idea of a spelling bee and incorporated it into every aspect of my campaign, from my video down to the descriptions of my perks. Even the lowest level incentive revolved around words, which still falls into the wide realm of a spelling bee.

Another example is the short film *Sync* by Brendon Fogle, which is about the relationship between a grandfather and his grandson and the connection they find through disconnection. The film revolves around the concept of nostalgia, specifically in the form of vinyl records. Brendon's campaign follows suit and reflects that concept, primarily in his perks and update videos.

Of course, there is also the element of surprise, or spontaneity, and those things can't be planned out in too much detail or too far in advance. But without a set strategy in place to afford you the luxury to be spontaneous when need be, the natural momentum and flow of the campaign could be threatened. Strategy and spontaneity should work together. The fine folks behind the feature-length film *Tilt* incorporated their backers into "*Tilt* the Town," which started out as a simple biography but morphed into something more immense than any of the campaign's 223 backers could have expected. What seemed to grow and prosper organically was partially planned out in some detail during the initial stages of their campaign, but it was also allowed to flourish into something much greater. (Don't worry, we'll examine the basic concept of *Tilt* the Town in the "Crowd Studies" section of this book.)

Maintaining your campaign is an important aspect of any crowd-funding endeavor, especially sustaining interest in it after you've reached your goal. Remember, the campaign's not finished just because you raised the funds and made your film. You've got contributors who are awaiting rewards and who are probably eager to see the finished film because, naturally, they're curious as to what their money helped to produce. It's also important to keep the same tone and demeanor you established at the beginning of your campaign right up until the end, since it will show your supporters that you are an organized person who knows the value of structure. More so, it'll show that you are fully focused on your film and its campaign, which helped bring the finished film one step closer to excellence.

Chapter Eleven

• • •

GIVE YOURSELF ENOUGH TIME

I'VE SEEN CAMPAIGNS raise upward of $5,000 in as little as two months like *Cerise* did, and I've seen other campaigns like *Iron Sky: The Coming Race* raise $500,000 within the same time frame. I've watched campaigns blast past the $1 million mark in a single day, and I've seen others rally up the indie film community support in those final fateful hours for a come-from-behind victory worthy of any underdog sports movie. Time is a delicate matter, and how much we need varies for each individual campaign. Therefore, you should take some time to decide on how much time you'll realistically need to raise the funds you're after.

Most crowdfunding platforms have parameters regarding how long a campaign can be active, which can range from a few weeks to a couple of months. But as Indiegogo's metrics suggest, more time does not always lead to more money. For *Cerise*'s campaign, I chose ninety days — back then, Indiegogo allowed campaigns to run for up to three months — because I thought that'd be a safe number, and through nonstop campaigning, my team and I were able to hit our $5,000 goal in two months.

That said, deciding how much time you're going to need to successfully crowdfund your film depends on a few factors, the first and most important being how much money you are looking to raise. Lower amounts ranging from a few hundred to a few thousand dollars will probably not need as much time as, say, a goal of $50,000 for a feature-length movie. But even this first factor depends heavily on two other factors: how large your current network is and how much of your own time you have to invest in campaigning.

Size matters, so the scope of your current network will play an integral role in deciding how long or short your campaign should be. I use the word "current" because once you start crowdfunding, your network will undoubtedly grow, especially from sharing your campaign on social media. If you've only started tweeting or finally created a Facebook page because "everyone else has one" and you've only got a handful of friends and followers, then raising substantial funds may be a bit more difficult. Not impossible, but more challenging than if you waited a few months to a year to build up not only your network but your credibility as a filmmaker and then launch your campaign when you've got a bit more clout or, at the very least, more than only your close friends following you on Twitter.

While a larger network will ultimately aid you toward a victorious campaign that much quicker, that victory also walks hand in hand with how much time you have to put into your campaign. Here I'll say it again: *Crowdfunding is a full-time job.* If you've already got a full-time job that's paying your bills and leaves hardly any time to eat and sleep, let alone time to maintain an active crowdfunding campaign, then raising $50,000 will be that much more difficult. Again, it's not impossible, but it will be more arduous than if you were working part-time at the neighborhood coffee shop and spending your downtime talking with your network about movies and your film campaign.

A successful campaign is one that doesn't sleep, but it also doesn't spend all of its time talking about itself; aside from mentioning your campaign a few times a day on the social sites and sending out an email once every few days, you also have to mingle with your potential contributors on a more personalized level. This is where all that time comes into play, but that's also where your team comes in to help. In terms of how much time you have available to devote to your campaign, you can take solace in the fact that there is no "I" in "team" — everyone on your team should participate and split the time it takes to keep active, both in crowd-funding and socializing. One thing to be aware of is that no one will give it the same 100% as you will, since, after all, it is *your* project and not theirs. However much time and effort is given to your campaign, rest assured that every bit will help to spread the word and bring in the funds.

Crowdfunding isn't a race to some imaginary finish line, so give yourself enough time, and, depending on how large your current network is and how much time you have to invest in campaigning, you should be able to choose a time frame that will best suit your individual campaign needs. But here's a statistic you cannot deny: According to Indiegogo's "New Research Study: 7 Stats from 100,000 Crowdfunding Campaigns," published on the Indiegogo Blog in October 2015, "of all the campaigns [Indiegogo] looked at that met their goals, nearly a third of them (30.5%) ran a campaign between 30 to 39 days long."

With all these basics covered and your "Way" plotted out before, it's time to delve into the actual running of your crowdfunding campaign. There is, however, a certain way of going to the crowd for help funding your film, and that's where *Crowdfunding for Filmmakers* really comes into play. The next section will open up before you a pathway that you can follow to a successful crowd-funding campaign, so that you will be able to make that film you keep playing in your head without worrying whether you can actually afford to make it. So let's begin to learn the Way to a successful film campaign.

• PART TWO •
SUMMARY POINTS

- Go with the *Tao* (Way) of traditional fundraising; the tools of the trade are the only difference between that and crowdfunding.

- The more skilled your teammates are, the smoother your campaign will run.

- Certain factors should be considered when deciding which crowdfunding platform you should run your campaign on, such as "All or Nothing" or "Keep What You Raise" fundraising models, the right tools, social media integration, and analytics.

- The size of your current network will play an important role in deciding how long your campaign should run and how much funding you should look to raise.

- Plan your campaign out as a strategy, leaving some room for spontaneity, as well.

• PART TWO •
EXERCISES

1. What is the logline of your film? Be succinct (short and on point). Is it a short film? Feature-length? Based on this, how much funding, at minimum, do you estimate you'll need to bring this film from script to screen? Write that number down.

2. Think about the audience of the film you want to crowdfund. What genre best fits the logline you wrote for it? Now, what niche(s) does your film fit into best? Is it made for a particular demographic? Basically, who are the people who are going to want to see your film once it's made?

3. If you don't already have one, set up a Twitter account. Start following film people (filmmakers, screenwriters, indie film influencers, and indie production and distribution companies), which can be found through a key word search. Then, start *interacting* with them, as well as tweeting interesting, relevant things to ensure a #followback from as many of them as possible.

PART
3

CAMPAIGN
PERSONALIZATION

Chapter Twelve

...

TE: INTEGRITY IS THE *TAO* TO (KA-) *CHING*!

WHOLENESS. INDIVISIBILITY. UNIFICATION. These are all words that describe the Taoist principle of *Te*, which literally translates to "integrity," or moral uprightness. When someone has a strong sense of moral principle, he or she knows something about him- or herself, and usually that something can't be compromised. How might this apply to crowdfunding for an indie film? In a single word: *personalization*.

One reason for the success of *Cerise* and many other crowdfunding campaigns like it is that it was engineered with one principle in mind: *Make everything about your audience.* The movie itself is the filmmaker's creation, and it's his or her passion that fuels the drive to launch and navigate a campaign to raise the funds to make it. It would be wonderful if all the people who contributed to your campaign did so simply to help an aspiring filmmaker soar to the top of his or her dreams and start a career in the entertainment industry, but that's not always the case. Many times, people contribute to a campaign because of what they will receive in return, and we as crowdfunders should be sensitive to this fact.

This is where the principle of *Te* can fit into various aspects of your campaign. The first and most important lesson it teaches us is humility, helping us realize that our campaigns are only partially about us and mostly about our potential contributors. We may have learned from TV commercials peddling products ranging from powerful gardening tools to OxiClean that selling something doesn't always work. Crowdfunding is not selling, although you are selling yourself to an extent and must therefore give some of yourself to your campaign and your backers. Of course, campaigns can be run in a very OxiClean fashion and still be successful, but where's the fun and creativity in that? More importantly, where's the connection between crowdfunder and contributor?

When I finished my campaign for *Cerise*, I penned a blog post called "Three Ps for a Successful Indie Film Campaign," those three Ps being pitch, perks, and promotion, and each had to be personalized in order to connect with an audience of potential contributors. Well, I've since simplified these principles, and they work much more in tandem with the concept of *Te*. After all, integrity is a trait best shown, not told.

The way to showcase *Te* during your crowdfunding campaign is to put some of yourself in every aspect of your campaign, not in a formal pitch, but an *invitation*; not by the quantity of your perks or rewards, but the quality of your *incentives*; and not through promotion of a campaign, but rather your *interactions* with friends and followers on social media. By going that extra mile in each of these "*three Ins*" and showing your potential contributors the real person behind your campaign, you become the very definition of integrity, a real *mensch*, and open yourself and your film to a brave new world of possibilities far exceeding the limits of the amount of dollars you'll raise through crowdfunding.

Chapter Thirteen

• • •

YOUR INVITATION VIDEO:
MAKE IT ABOUT YOUR FILM
AND YOURSELF

FIRST IMPRESSIONS ARE everything. That's why the most important aspect of your crowdfunding campaign is the campaign or pitch video, which I will refer to as the *invitation*. It's usually the first thing anyone sees after typing your campaign's link into a browser. Before we delve into what an invitation really is, it's important we take a quick look at a few things that are *not* invitations:

• Photographs, no matter how expertly shot they are

• A movie's trailer, no matter how compelling it is

• Behind-the-scenes and/or interview footage

Although the cliché is true, that a picture speaks a thousand words, the chances that it'll speak those words eloquently enough to get someone to part with a hard-earned $20 bill are slim. The trailer for a film is a sales tool geared to get people to want to see your film. And as humorous and insightful as behind-the-scenes and interview footage can be, rarely will it make anyone want to contribute to your film's campaign, especially if you're staring off at a twenty-degree angle toward an imaginary interviewer talking about how awesome your film is going to be.

When I pieced together my invitation video for *Cerise*, I wasn't exactly sure how to go about it. I did some research, naturally, and I watched a lot of videos, many of which didn't impress me. Some were interesting, and they all spoke to me, the viewer, about a particular project and how integral my support would be to getting it made, but the majority of them didn't make me want to plug in my debit card digits and join the cause. I decided to try something different with my video. I got together with Marinell and Alain and shot some footage, which I edited the following week and then uploaded the full video to YouTube. I launched the campaign, but before I sent out my first tweet, I became hesitant, besieged by doubts and questions: *Who's gonna want to help me make my film? Is this campaign video any good? Why am I even doing this?*

And as I was about to click the "Delete" button and go make *Cerise* the way I'd made my other seven films, with my own money, I saw on Twitter that @Indiegogo had mentioned me in a tweet urging its followers to check out the Project of the Day, *Cerise*, with its "awesome pitch clip." It seems my video had a fan who had taken it upon herself (I'd find out later that this fan was none other than co-founder Danae Ringelmann) to start the promotion for me while I was basking in the cold shadow of doubt and fear of failure. That's when I realized just how much potential my invitation video's fun nature and personal touch could have in crowdfunding my film.

13.1. *This scene from* Cerise's *campaign video shows potential backers just how much love we'd express to an associate producer.*

Essentially, your campaign video is the one and only chance you have to really sell *yourself*, not necessarily your project. Take some time to talk to your potential contributors. Tell them about yourself, and then tell them why you want to make this film and why they should be the ones to make it happen. Again, keep in mind the "they" of this whole enterprise. We may think crowdfunding is about us, but the word "I" is only a tiny letter in the word; the bulk of it is "crowd," so make it about the crowd.

The Anatomy of an Invitation

A personal invitation like the one for *Cerise* and many other successful campaigns can be broken into four key parts: the *introduction*, the *invitation* itself, the *showcase*, and the *call of action*.

The introduction is your opportunity to make the acquaintance of your potential contributors and let them know a little about who you are not only as a filmmaker, but as a person. It's your chance to quickly connect with your future contributors. My introduction consisted of letting people know the three most important things about me: I'm a poet, filmmaker, and freelance professor (at the time). That's it. Keep your introduction as short and on-point as possible.

Once you conclude your introduction, it's time to turn the attention to your actual invitation, which can also be broken into three parts: the *summary*, *purpose*, and *incentives*. The shortest form of a summary in filmmaking is the logline, which is traditionally kept at one or two concise sentences that encapsulate the bulk of what your story is about. Think of it as a brief overview of your film. This is followed by the purpose of the campaign, in which you tell your potential contributors why you're raising funds for your film through crowdfunding, what those funds will be used for, and any other pertinent information that addresses the "why" of your campaign. After that, it's typically a good idea to briefly mention some of the incentives that people will get in exchange for their monetary contribution to your film campaign. Granted, I went the extra yard with my invitation for *Cerise* and shot short scenes to illustrate those perks on offer at each of my perk levels, but not all campaign videos have to be this detailed.

The next part of an invitation is the showcase, which is where you build your credibility as a filmmaker by showing samples of your prior film work and highlighting any awards and recognition you or your work may have received. You've already built up the *Te* necessary to get viewers of your video to listen to you through your introduction and invitation, but now you need to show them you know your way around an ALEXA 65 and a film set. In my video for *Cerise*, I showcased a few shots from some of the shorts I'm most proud of, as well as a sitcom pilot I directed that won two awards (at the time, four altogether) for excellence in filmmaking. What better way to build up your potential contributors' confidence in your current film than with some film festival recognition for your previous work?

Finally, there's the call of action, because, much the way an actor will not get into character and start reciting his or her lines until the director yells "Action!" your crowd may not necessarily know what you expect them to do once they finish watching your campaign video. At best, they might be intrigued and certainly feel invited into something. But *what*, exactly? Call to them, and tell them what they need to do next to help you make your next indie film.

SMILE — YOU'RE ON CAMERA (OR SHOULD BE)

A mistake that many crowdfunders make is not starring in their campaign videos. The truth is you *must* be in your video. As I mentioned earlier, there are not too many people out there who will give money to a photograph or a movie trailer, let alone to a ghost, and that's what you become to potential contributors when you don't appear in your video. People give to people, and while it's true that no one likes to ask others for money, by choosing to crowdfund, that's exactly what you're doing, and the least you can do for these individuals is ask them as personally as possible to join the campaign. In this case, your campaign video is as personal as it's going to get.

A story I love to tell about the importance of being in your campaign video is one about friend and filmmaker Jeanie Finlay and her campaign for *Sound It Out*, a documentary about the last record shop in Teesside, UK. I originally made her acquaintance when she asked if I'd give her some feedback on her Indiegogo. I watched her video, which was really just a trailer for the film. I told her she needed to be in the video and ask people directly to join the campaign rather than having them read the story below. She decided to keep it as is and launched her campaign to raise the funds needed to finish *Sound It Out*.

A few weeks later, I received a tweet from Jeanie with a link. It seems she had not been raising very much money during the opening weeks of her campaign, so she reconsidered my advice and recorded a new video, this time with her in it. Practically overnight she saw a substantial difference. Funds started rolling in through tons of promotion on her part, and when all was said and done, she'd overshot her initial goal of $3,000 by $1,468! Now *Sound It Out* has screened at film festivals all over the world, including the well-known Sheffield Doc Fest, Silverdocs, and Edinburgh International Film Festival.

Jeanie then recorded another campaign video with her once again taking center stage when she launched a second successful Indiegogo campaign for $5,000 to get her and her team to the highly prestigious SXSW, where *Sound It Out* had its world premiere. And after that, Jeanie went on to record a third video to bring *Sound It Out* to theaters across the United Kingdom.

13.2. *That's Jeanie Finlay starring in her campaign video for her feature-length documentary* Sound It Out.

This time, she partnered with Sheffield Doc Fest and brought in $828 over her $10,000 goal. That's over $20,000 in crowdfunding between three campaigns with three very personal invitations at the forefront of Jeanie's multiple successes.

TIME IS OF THE ESSENCE, AND TIME IS SHORT

One thing to keep in mind is *time*. Even though we're living in a world where most people are more oriented to visual images over words, attention spans are diminishing at an alarming rate. An invitation video, therefore, should be as short as possible, and I suggest a runtime of between two and three minutes at most. Anything longer, such as full synopses, director's statements, and other stories about what inspired the film, can be added to the story beneath your campaign video. Your incentives will be listed in greater detail to the right of the video, keeping the video itself as a short, sweet, and simple introduction to you, your film, and your abilities as a filmmaker just before you call them to "Action!" and compel them to bring your next great masterpiece to the world.

Chapter Fourteen

• • •

Incentives: Make Them About Your Film and Its Contributors

THE REAL MUSCLES behind crowdfunding are the incentives and the fundamental concept that if you give me money, you get something in return. And while there's nothing wrong with offering what I call *standard definition* incentives, which are the more typical merchandise like T-shirts, digital downloads, DVD and Blu-ray copies of the finished film, signed posters, PDF scripts, and associate and executive producer credit in your film, it's much better to think outside the money box and get *Hi-Def* (experiential) and *3-D!* (personal) with your incentives. Examples of each include experiences like advance tickets to red-carpet screenings and customized voice-mail greetings recorded by one of the actors in your film.

Let's have a look at these three types of crowdfunding incentives in more detail.

STANDARD DEFINITION (MANDATORY) INCENTIVES

Standard definition incentives are exactly what it says — standard. I also call these "mandatory merch" because they are the kinds of items your audience will most likely expect to receive. If they're funding a film campaign, they expect a copy of the film they're funding. Things like signed scripts and posters, mugs, T-shirts, and any other merchandise you can emblazon with your film's title and sell are all standard. If you think your audience will want them, offer them.

The most important thing here is to price these items accordingly, keeping in mind the phrase "more value for less money." There's a perceived value to each of these items; as I mentioned earlier, a DVD isn't worth a $50 bill, but one signed by the director and the cast now has added value. A digital download is not worth $25 (at the time of this writing, the iTunes standard price for a Hollywood movie was $14.99), but a live stream of the film a week before its official release? That's certainly worth $25, because it gives early access to your contributors for opting in long before the film's finished.

Now, if you can get away with keeping your standard definition perks digital only, you'll find yourself in a much better place when fulfillment time comes around, when you need to deliver on all the perks you promised. I learned the hard way how expensive a run of 100 T-shirts can be, which is why you'll see most T-shirts on crowdfunding sites going for $65 and up. But if you don't sell a certain number of those shirts, you ultimately will lose some funding that could be going to your film because you'll still need to fulfill T-shirts or mugs at 500 units or 5 units.

HI-DEF (EXPERIENTIAL) INCENTIVES

High definition (Hi-Def/HD or experiential) incentives go the extra mile for your potential contributors. They give them access to experiences they otherwise would not be given if it weren't for this crowdfunding campaign for your film. Again, these are things like advance screenings of your film, visits to the set, and even getting killed on screen by a Tyrannosaurus Rex. (Yes, that last one is a real perk — just ask the filmmakers behind the campaign for *Iron Sky: The Coming Race.*)

One of the greatest examples of Hi-Def access like no other is the Indiegogo for *Life Itself*, the documentary about the life of Roger Ebert. Through strategic partnerships with VHX, a premiere online distribution platform, and the Sundance Film Festival, where the film had its world premiere, the filmmakers were able to offer their Indiegogo backers the chance to screen the film at home while the film premiered in Park City, Utah — something that had never been done before. And how much did the campaign owners behind *Life Itself*'s campaign charge for this privilege, you ask? Only $25 got you a code to stream the film live from Sundance, so it's no wonder they sold 474 of the "Pre-Theatrical Stream" perks alone.

One thing you want to do is keep up-to-date with the changing trends and technologies of the time, especially as it pertains to crowdfunding and filmmaking. For instance, once upon a time a Skype conversation with the film's director was a high-value Hi-Def perk. But Skype, and even Google Hangouts to an extent, are not as cutting edge as they used to be and are quickly being replaced by broadcast platforms like Periscope, Meerkat, and even Hang w/, which Alan Tudyk and Nathan Fillion used exclusively to connect with their fans and backers during their Indiegogo for their geek-centric web series *Con Man*. You would want to offer up those in place of the more old-school methods of live streaming that are not as relevant today as they were yesterday.

3-D! (PERSONALIZED) INCENTIVES

I've only ever seen three movies in 3-D — one good, and one not so good, and one whose 3-D effects didn't add much to the movie. The good one was James Cameron's *Avatar*. I was completely immersed in every facet of the film. Most recently I saw *Star Wars: The Force Awakens* in IMAX 3-D, then I saw it in 2-D. The third dimension didn't help make Episode VII any better than it naturally is. The not-so-good one I watched was 2011's *Green Lantern* movie starring Ryan Reynolds, and that's probably all I need to say about that.

The difference is that with *Avatar*, I was pulled into a story so strange and magnificent that I couldn't help but marvel at all the fantastical elements of Pandora bursting with life all around me. The way a good 3-D movie brings you into the world of the film, so does a good 3-D! crowdfunding incentive pull you deeper into the world of the movie you're seeking funding for.

A timeless example of a 3-D! incentive is *Cerise*'s acrostic poem perk, which isn't even listed on the campaign. Originally, I only offered a social media shout-out at the $10 level. When I saw it wasn't selling well, Marinell suggested I write each backer a poem at the $10 level and up, since I'm a poet and *Cerise* is a

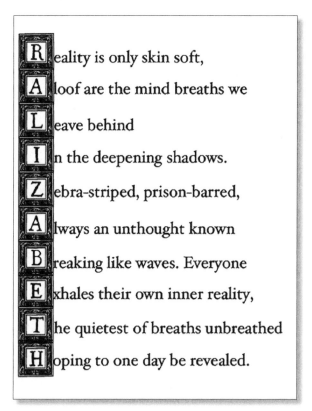

R eality is only skin soft,

A loof are the mind breaths we

L eave behind

I n the deepening shadows.

Z ebra-striped, prison-barred,

A lways an unthought known

B reaking like waves. Everyone

E xhales their own inner reality,

T he quietest of breaths unbreathed

H oping to one day be revealed.

14.1. *The acrostic poem I wrote for "Ralizabeth," in which every line starts with a letter of her name.*

film about words. After a little protest — I was worried I'd have to write fifty poems — I decided to write each of my backers a poem using the most important word they'll ever have: their own names. This forged an instant connection to *Cerise* and to myself. And for the record, I ended writing over 100 of these personalized poems, and it was worth every line.

Years later, I still see some contributors, now friends of mine, using the poems I wrote for them as their profile pictures all across social media, since Marinell formatted each one in Photoshop so that we could then post them on every backer's Facebook wall individually.

Another Indiegogo that offered a similar 3-D! perk is the one for *Twenty Million People*, a feature-length film by Michael Ferrell, Devin Sanchez, and Chris Pine. At the $25 contribution level, Michael would write his backers a choose-your-own-adventure-style romantic comedy. *Twenty Million People* centers on the idea that it's difficult to find that special someone in the midst of a city twenty million people strong. Michael, the film's writer and director, would draft up a first act in second-person narration and offer you a choice at the end of it. Once you figure out how you'd like to proceed, he'd then write a second act based around that decision and give you one final choice to make that will lead to a well-deserved denouement of your making.

What's also great about this particular incentive is that it fits in with the overall theme of the film. In fact, over 100 of the campaign's 137 backers chose incentives at $25 and above. That's over 100 rom-coms written and over 100 funders who now have a deeper connection to Michael's film because they are part of the "twenty million people" who make up the title of the film.

Around Here, a science-fiction film by Tim Sparks about an Afghanistan war veteran who finds solace in an extraordinary encounter in Colorado, is another prime example of a campaign that goes the distance for its contributors. For a $20 contribution, Tim would write and record a brief ukulele song for his backers. Granted, there may be no ukulele score in *Around Here* when it's done, but Tim gives us a glimpse into his world, not only as a film-maker crowdfunding his latest movie, but also as a musician.

I've given you a lot of examples of 3-D! incentives because they are the most difficult ones to come up with when planning out an indie film's crowdfunding campaign, but they are the most impor-tant kind of rewards to offer. Even I fell into the black-and-white world of mundane incentives. Many of *Cerise*'s perks are pretty standard definition with a few Hi-Def ones thrown in: At the $50 level, I offered a T-shirt that says "I spelt *Cerise*" and a signed copy of the DVD; at $100, contributors could visit the set as an associate producer (and enjoy a classic Jersey meal on me at a local diner, which is borderline personal since I offer a small bit of myself, with my being Greek and New Jersey being the diner capital of the world); and at $500, contributors not only got awarded the title of executive producer, but they also received an invitation to a private screening of *Cerise* in New York City.

It's important to keep a couple of things in mind. First, the film you're crowdfunding probably won't be the last film you ever make, which means you'll need funding for future projects, and crowdfunding will certainly be an option, especially in the wake of the JOBS Act and equity crowdfunding (see Chapter Thirty-Six). Second, you're not only crowdfunding for funds, but you're crowdsourcing an audience as well, and by creating a personal connection with your contributors, they will be more likely to contribute to another of your subsequent campaigns. So the ques-tion to ask yourself really isn't how much you want to make this particular film, but how much you want to be a filmmaker.

Remastered (in High Definition)

Once you find out what the phrase "Go Hi-Def or go home" actually means and how time-consuming getting personal actually is, you'll understand why a lot of campaigners choose to stick to standard definition incentives, especially in the midst of a day job, family obligations, house chores, and just having a social life. But you get out what you put in with crowdfunding an indie film, so I recommend you give more of yourself to get the most for your film.

Now, I may not believe that restored Hi-Def digital transfers make much difference in all those old films I prefer over today's fast-paced CGI spectaculars, but I definitely believe that not all of your incentives have to be 100% 3-D! If there's just one portion of your rewards that offers contributors a bit of insight into you as a person and filmmaker, or that makes them feel more deeply connected to you and your film, then any standard definition incentive becomes all the more valuable.

Personalization can be as simple as being yourself. Take, for example, the Kickstarter for *This Is Ours*, a feature-length film by Kris and Lindy Boustedt about a couple on the verge of divorce who head to their summer house one last time, where they encounter a pair of free spirits who embody the tradition of the great American landscape. Right at the top of their rewards list? For $1, they'll not only give you a thank-you shout-out on the *This Is Ours* Facebook page (standard definition and ordinary), but they'll shout your name from their front porch in the middle of the day (3-D! and extraordinary).

The gurus of geek behind the Kickstarter for *Nintendo Quest*, a film documenting the cross-country journey of Jay Bartlett on his quest to piece together a complete official North American NES collection, offer the film's 8-bit soundtrack to their fans on cassette.

Again, the ordinary (film's soundtrack) becomes extraordinary by means of the relevant medium it's recorded on (the cassette tape).

Lastly, make your incentives about your contributors. Think about the most beloved holidays in the US, like Christmas, Valentine's Day, and Easter. As much as we'd like to think they're all about giving, they're really not. People like to receive things. Yes, some people do contribute without much care about what they'll get in return, but these altruistic Bruce Wayne types come around once in a dark night. You will ultimately receive a tweet or email from a contributor asking where that T-shirt he paid for is or when she'll get the DVD she spent $50 on. This is all fine and normal. Crowdfunding is about the crowd, after all.

Chapter Fifteen

• • •

INTERACTIONS: IT'S NOT ABOUT YOU, IT'S ABOUT *US*

ACTUALLY, LET'S TAKE a step back for a second, shall we?

When I wrote the first edition of *Crowdfunding for Filmmakers*, this chapter was initially called "Promotion: Make It Your Whole World (and Everyone Else's, Too!)" Back then, and up until 2014, that's what we did when we launched a crowdfunding campaign — we promoted, or marketed, our campaigns to our social networks. And people still promote their campaigns today, but the question is *to whom*? The truth is you need to build an audience *before* you start marketing your film to them, and the only way to do that in a social media–driven culture is to *interact* with them first.

This opening act of crowdfunding an indie film is what I call *crowdfinding* because you have to find the crowd before you can ask them to fund something. It's just like when you attend a live taping of a late-night talk show like *The Late Show with Stephen Colbert*. Before taping begins, a comedian is sent out to warm the crowd up and get them laughing loudly so the microphones can record genuine, loud laughter. Sure, we're here to see Stephen, but the opening act is what gets us comfortable enough to participate in the live laugh track. With crowdfunding an indie film, the word "interaction" really takes the place of two words — *community building* — because community fuels the beat that keeps the heart of crowdfunding an indie film pumping.

FIND FIRST, FUND FASTER: BUILDING AN AUDIENCE

Before we get into interactions while you're crowdfunding your next indie film, let's talk about what needs to be done before the crowdfunding starts. Like the word itself, the "crowd" comes before the "funding," so the first thing I recommend is starting a Facebook page and Twitter account for your film a few weeks to a couple of months before you even think about crowdfunding, and start talking with fans and followers about similar interests, like movies and making them. If you read an article about the latest DSLR on the market, share that article. I have a personal rule: If you read it, tweet it. Learn from the people you follow as much as they'll learn from every bit of value you give them in the form of a tweet or a status update. For help with this aspect of social media, I recommend downloading a copy of *Social Media Charm School*, a swift and enjoyable read by Julie Keck and Jessica King, who truly understand what kind of work and fun goes into building audiences for indie films.

What you will ultimately discover is that the more you interact with people, the more invested they become in *you*, not only as a filmmaker, but also as a person (that's where the "charm" comes in). Or they may come to view you as an authority on a particular topic you tweet a lot about, or about a certain director or genre of film. Perhaps you're an advocate of #womenfilmmakers on Twitter and choose to promote films that are made by an all-female crew. Perhaps, like me, you're a thought leader in the space of crowdfunding for film. Whatever it is, own it and keep up the relevant interactions that come with it.

Now, once you get into a flow and rhythm of interacting with your followers on a regular basis, and once you've gotten used to giving value in every tweet, status update, and even email update you send out, then you will appreciate the art and science behind promoting your crowdfunding campaign. Go all in, and showcase your *Te* early on; before you start asking your crowd for anything, you want to give them your everything.

THE SOCIAL PSYCHOLOGY OF CROWDFUNDING

When I was a senior in high school, I took a class called Mass Media, and our teacher, Mr. Colasurdo, spent a great deal of time making us read a textbook about persuasion and various other methods the media use to create a need in people. Not much of it sank in until Mr. Colasurdo started demonstrating these principles by having us analyze TV commercials. He would help us to see how particular commercials used psychology to make us believe that we need to only use Tide if we cared about our family's clean, fresh clothing, or to choose Wheaties over other cereals because our favorite sports player chooses this brand over Frosted Flakes.

As with just about anything else in the world, marketing can make or break a great new product. Today, marketing and advertising are at their most creative, and they are becoming more and more personalized toward the consumers whose attention they are trying to capture. In order to do this, there's a great deal of psychology at work in every ad we see. Catchy phrases like "Roll that beautiful bean footage" from the Bush's Baked Beans commercials are being replaced with concept videos that have more depth, like Chevrolet's "Chevy Runs Deep" campaign.

And marketing has continued to evolve from snazzy slogans to universal concepts. Today especially in our app-driven culture, everything is about us, and while we may think services like Uber and Lyft are selling us a ride when we open up the app on our phone and order one, social media expert Gary Vaynerchuck would argue that they're selling something more valuable to us than a simple ride. They're selling us *time* — time saved in a world in which we never seem to have enough. These companies don't even need to advertise because it's all word of mouth, right from the people who saved that time they may have otherwise wasted waiting for a subway or hailing a taxi.

Uber and Lyft sell us something more personal than a ride. Chevrolet sells us something more meaningful than just a Volt or Blazer. Bush's doesn't sell us on a tasty brand of baked beans, but on the legacy of a family recipe that Jay tries desperately to keep a secret while his dog Duke is determined to make millions selling it off to the highest bidder. Today more than ever, people don't just want to buy a car, they want to buy into a legacy. A story. Author Michael Margolis demonstrates this concept best in his book *Believe Me*, in which he writes about the notebook company Moleskine. Not many writers would pay $10 plus tax to buy a standard black hardcover journal when they can get a $2 softcover one with more pages at the neighborhood supermarket. There's really nothing all that special about Moleskine *except* its tradition of being the "legendary notebooks of van Gogh, Matisse, and Hemingway." That's what we're buying into when writers buy a Moleskine journal or Cahier. It's not just a notebook, it's a legend.

All of this is an interaction, a dialogue between a company creatively promoting their products and the passionate consumers who buy them. By making their products about higher concept ideas, these companies allow you to interact with them; if you buy that Moleskine notebook that was used by the legends of old, you might become just as legendary one day. This is the key to connecting properly with your audience when you're crowd-funding an independent film.

CONNECT AUDIENCES TO YOUR FILM AND YOURSELF

These same tactics employed in marketing a product should be employed to raise awareness about your crowdfunding campaign. It should keep up with the trends of the time, and in this case, marketing is all about personalization. You're not simply spreading the word about your film campaign, you're putting yourself out there as well, and therefore, it's important to market yourself with your campaign because, by default, you make your campaign more personal that way.

Many times, contributors will support a campaign solely because they feel connected to the person behind it; either they know this person directly or they get a positive vibe from him or her based on the project's campaign video. The quality of the film may not even matter at that point because the crowdfunder has sold him- or herself as filmmaker on this particular project, making it mean something more to his or her contributors. In other instances, contributors support projects because they're high concept, they look humorous or interesting, or they revolve around subjects that are long overdue for big and small screens alike. Whatever the reason contributors have for backing your film campaign, it's up to you to convince them it's a worthwhile film to put their money behind.

Rock It Around the Clock

It's no secret that a successful crowdfunding campaign demands around-the-clock connection to people's attention. We get tired of seeing the same commercial repeatedly, but at the end of your prime-time entertainment, you remember that commercial whether you want to or not, unless you changed the channel. In today's technocracy, this translates to constant tweets, relentless Facebook status updates, personalized emails, sleep strikes, the occasional hunger strike, and any other means by which to keep your film campaign on the minds of your friends, family, supporters, contributors, and potential contributors. This is really what makes a film campaign a full-time job.

There are two surefire ways to make your campaign a *fool*-time job, and that is to do little or no promotion whatsoever or to do little to no interacting with your audience outside of the standard style of promotion. A static campaign, or one that is all about marketing without interactions, will end on the same number it started out with, and that's zero. Shakespeare expressed it best in the words of King Lear: "Nothing will come from nothing." No updates, no comments, no value will result in no money for your film campaign and a bad taste in your mouth about crowdfunding that wouldn't be there had you done it right from the launch. You have to work hard to get what you want. If you want this funding, you should be showing people your desire in every way you can. You need to be honest and proactive, and only then will you find an audience who cares about you and your film enough to help you make it happen.

THERE WILL BE REJECTION

I'm sure many beginning crowdfunders are concerned about the rejection that could result from a film campaign with a strong Internet and social media presence. No one likes to wake up one morning to the realization that yesterday he or she had 2,005 friends on Facebook and this morning that number dwindled down to 1,996. But as Twitter and Facebook gain credibility as marketing and advertising tools for companies, so will it be the case amongst various communities of artists. I've already grown accustomed to seeing five to ten different film campaigns being shared by my friends and followers all along this brave new social landscape.

But yes, if you overdo the promotional aspect of crowdfunding and cross the line into spam territory, you will lose friends and followers and will even be asked by some people on your email list to remove them from further emails — take it from me because it happened to me. Or, you could attract even more people, as was the case with me as well. It all depends on whether you create and maintain a strategy to keep your interactions and promotions in proper balance, but we'll discuss more of that in Chapters Twenty-Eight and Twenty-Nine.

By combining intense yet distinctive interactions with your audience, unique incentives, and a compelling invitation, you'll have yourself a winning triumvirate. The spirit of these should be all you, and if you give to those potential contributors a piece of you, they'll give you more than just a piece of their paycheck. They'll give you the power you need to *really* succeed.

Chapter Sixteen

. . .

THE ELEMENTS OF STYLE: DRESSING YOUR CAMPAIGN FOR SUCCESS

THERE'S AN OLD piece of advice I heard once, and although I can't recall where or from whom I heard it, it somehow worked its way into my first film: Dress for the job you want, not for the job you have.

Now, while this may not necessarily be true today from a careers perspective, it has become more prevalent where crowdfunding is concerned. An indie film campaign should always strive to serve as an extension of the movie you're looking to produce. And since a campaign is partially about building up integrity that the film is worth giving funding to, then for the sake of that *Te* we owe it to ourselves to take time and dress our campaigns in their Sunday best for maximum success.

When I crowdfunded *Cerise*, it was fine to have a campaign story that was all or mostly text. But as crowdfunding evolves and more and more film campaigns must compete with one another to attract potential contributors, focusing on design and media will become increasingly important to make those campaigns dynamic and compelling. That said, here are a few style tips for setting up a dynamic campaign that sells itself with style and class.

DESIGN AROUND YOUR STORY

One of the easiest ways to add some color to your campaign's story is to add images. There are a few ways of doing this; one is simply putting photos of varying sizes into a campaign page and calling it a day. There are still plenty of examples of successful campaigns that go this simple route — from short film campaigns like Michael Bekemeyer's Kickstarter for *Impasse* to campaigns raising funds for a film's theatrical release like *Radio Free Albemuth*.

However, the same way you might not throw on a button-down shirt over a tee to attend a very formal cocktail party, you should button up those visual assets in your campaign with the finer detail of *design*, like the filmmakers behind *What Lola Wants* did with their Indiegogo, as well as the filmmakers of *Star Trek: Captain Pike* (kept a *Star Trek* theme intact, right down to the pie chart) and *Ghost in the Gun* (section headers add a western feel to match the film's story and tone).

A well-dressed campaign takes time, so take that time to create headers with Photoshop instead of bolding section headings. Craft images for each of your perks, and make sure they're all on brand with the look and feel of the indie film you're crowdfunding.

KEEP UP WITH THE STYLE OF THE TIME

Unless you're making a period piece. Then, keep it period. An indie film campaign should keep up with crowdfunding trends. That may mean something as simple as CAPITALIZING all of the incentives in your perks or rewards column so they stand out to potential contributors perusing at a quick glance, or a tad more complex like adding an anchor text to your campaign's HTML code so your audience in France can read all about your film campaign in their own language.

KEEP TEXT TRIM AND NEAT

As soon as I wake up each morning, the first thing I do is read a single verse of the *Tao Te Ching* because each of its 82 verses is just short enough for me to get through in less than a minute of reading time. But the value is immeasurable! We're filmmakers for a reason, so chances are we probably don't read as much as we'd like to, and chances are that our audiences don't either. That said, be sure that you use as little black text on white background as possible. If a single image can take the place of a block of paragraph, go with the image. If you absolutely need the words to expand on something in (a *little*) more detail, since "brevity is the soul of wit," do as Polonius does in *Hamlet* and be brief (and even he's not all that brief).

STAND OUT IN A CROWD

When I attend events and film festivals, speaking events, and mixers, I make sure I stand out by wearing a blazer and a fedora or a pork pie. With a campaign, this pertains mostly to social media: Make sure we can find you on Twitter and Facebook easily. If your platform of choice has a section for easily telling people where else they might find your campaign, like Indiegogo does, then make sure you connect your social media properly. If not, work it into the campaign text. This enhances the trust factor (see the next chapter for more about that) and builds up your integrity factor, too.

DON'T SKIMP ON THE ACCESSORIES

Like a good-looking pie chart. Just how a proper pocket square or a feather in a fedora can complete even a purposefully unkempt style of dress, a proper pie chart detailing what you'll do with the funds you raise is a must-have accessory in crowdfunding. It's easy to find a standard Microsoft Office–style "bored room"–grade pie chart and fill in the details, but something standard in a campaign that's alive with some flair already will only dim that campaign's visual shine and make it seem less than kempt. Get creative with your pie charts like these filmmakers did for their horror film *Found Footage 3-D.*

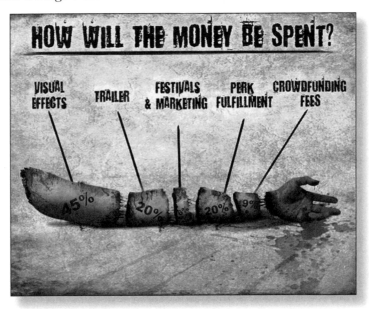

DON'T FORGET TO BE SOCIAL

While you're hard at work creating those headers, images for incentives, and pie charts in Photoshop to add some color to your campaign's story, don't forget to create promotional materials for your film's Facebook and Twitter pages. A cover photo is prime real estate, and once we look at your page, we should immediately know that you're running a crowdfunding campaign for your indie film.

Using the main branding for your movie, plus the logo of your crowdfunding platform of choice, as well as the short link to your campaign, any relevant hashtags or taglines, and perhaps the duration dates, you can inform visitors to your page — friends, followers, and even random people who may have just sent you a friend request or given you a follow — that you have a campaign running on Indiegogo or Kickstarter. Michael Dougherty did it brilliantly for the Indiegogo for his zombie film *Z★Con*:

ALWAYS WEAR THE HAT

Never let the hat wear you. From a crowdfunding standpoint, this means you should be proud to metaphorically wear your campaign anywhere you go and talk about how awesome it, and your film, is with confidence. This way, when you show someone at a cocktail party your campaign from your smartphone, or give them a campaign card so they can check it out later, all the talk you're doing about it won't be all hype, but an impression, and first impressions are everything.

Chapter Seventeen

"Be Water, My Friend... " — Transparency Is Clear and Cool

Immortal martial artist, actor, and philosopher Bruce Lee spent much time perfecting himself in the physical world, as evidenced by some of his greatest films like *Enter the Dragon* and *Fist of Fury*, but also within the spiritual realm by studying various philosophies like Taoism and Buddhism. It's clear that Lee understood the importance of flow in the physical and ethereal planes, and it was with this in mind that he spoke what has become one of his most meaningful quotations:

> "Be formless... shapeless, like water. Now you put water into a cup, it becomes the cup. You pour water into a bottle; it becomes the bottle. You put water into a teapot; it becomes the teapot. Now water can flow, or creep or drip or crash! Be water, my friend... "

In the crowdfunding plane, you are the water, so pour yourself into it fully, and in the same way you would pour yourself into a film or screenplay. As I mentioned before, filmmakers often rush into crowdfunding with the sole idea that it is a hassle. They'd rather be working on their films, sketching storyboards, or creating shot lists. All of this will happen in due time, but if your mind is on something other than the task at hand, that task will be compromised. Sometimes we take the shape of a director, other times a cinematographer, perhaps, but whatever we do, in order to do it right, we must allow ourselves to fill in every crevice of that title or job description and give that particular job 100% of ourselves for the time being.

Flow is a much more important aspect of crowdfunding than most people realize. Soon after you set up your campaign, personalize your invitation and incentives, launch your campaign, and start interacting with others about it, you'll notice whether all is going well. That's flow. If your campaign is faltering a short time into it, you should probably question why. Most of the time it's because you, the crowdfunder, are not putting all of yourself into campaigning. Perhaps you're working a day job, which is a reasonable necessity. You may have family to take care of, which, again, is another understandable necessity. You may enjoy sleep, which is again understandable. But the fact is that if you're pouring yourself into a few different glasses all at once, none of those glasses can ever hope to become filled with the potential they deserve because you only have so much water to give.

Going with the flow means necessity, and crowdfunding should become, at least for the days or months you're doing it, just as important a necessity as work and family and sleep. Crowdfunding for your film must become the glass that gets filled closest to the top. Like Bruce Lee says, "Water can flow or it can crash," and a surefire way to make it crash is to try to do too much with the limited time you have to crowdfund your film.

Water not only flows and takes the shape of the thing it's poured into, but it's also transparent, and *transparency* is perhaps the most essential component of crowdfunding. It allows people to see what's happening on the screen and behind the scenes, and as Gary Vaynerchuk says, "Trust is on the rise because transparency is on the rise." When crowdfunding, you may get questions like "Is my transaction secure?" and "What happens if you don't hit your goal?" Most of these are easily answered in your platform's "Help Center" since those platforms are taking steps every day to ensure contributors *feel* safe. However, you as the campaign's owner should know what the *contribution flow* of your preferred platform is like so you can answer those questions as they may arise, thus building up your trust factor, too.

And trust is a two-way street (or river, rather). On the contributor side of things, platforms are working to ensure that they feel confident giving to campaigns. Indiegogo, for instance, has a "Trust Passport," which asks campaigners to verify their email and connect via Facebook and/or LinkedIn to help build up that trust and transparency, so essential to contributors, who deserve to know if that person they're giving their hard-earned money to is worthy of that trust.

Since crowdfunding is online fundraising, most of the funds you receive from contributors will be made online. What happens if you bring a little money in from a friend who isn't especially tech-savvy and doesn't want to contribute to your campaign online, and instead hands you $100 in cash or as a check? How do you report that to your online contributors? It's easy — you just let them know.

When I crowdfunded *Cerise*, I raised a very small amount of money from external sources, namely a couple of former students of mine, one who contributed $10 and another who contributed a slightly more substantial amount. The first thing I learned is that you should be honest about receiving funds in this way. Granted, there's really no way for your contributors to find out that you brought in additional money behind the scenes unless you tell them, but by doing so, your integrity as a crowdfunder stays intact and you show yourself to be sincere and trustworthy with other people's money.

Nowadays, you can actually add any additional amounts of money you raise separately from your online campaigning on most crowdfunding platforms, and even attribute that contribution to the person who gave it, so it's much easier to keep your campaigning as clear as water. The minute we do something as crowdfunders that puts us under the scrutiny of our supporters and contributors, it's very difficult to rebound. Again, it's about keeping your *Te* intact for this and any future crowdfunding endeavors, and that means bending when the road before you bends instead of trying too hard to continue straight ahead. In short, you should always go with the natural flow of crowdfunding to avoid any possible pitfalls and plummets along the way.

Chapter Eighteen

• • •

A PRACTICAL GUIDE TO CROWDFUNDER ETIQUETTE

SOME OF YOU might be thinking, *I didn't know such a thing as crowd-funder etiquette existed!* Well, it does or doesn't, depending on your own experiences with crowdfunding and/or contributing to a campaign or ten. I prefer to call it by its more common name, *good manners*, and here are a few basic tenets every campaigner should strive to uphold.

THANK YOUR CONTRIBUTORS

A good friend of mine who had successfully crowdfunded his feature-length film brought this to my attention as one of his pet peeves. He mentioned that he had contributed to a few campaigns, and the filmmakers didn't even tweet a simple "thank you" for his contributions. I couldn't believe it. I thought to myself, *Would someone really not thank a complete stranger for giving money to his or her campaign?* Apparently, the answer is yes, and it's audacious (and will most surely end one's future as a crowdfunder).

As a crowdfunder, thank each and every contributor to your film campaign, whether he or she pitched in $500 or $5. It's really the absolute least you can do to show your appreciation for coming to bat for your film and for you. Sending an email, a message on Facebook, and/or a direct message on Twitter is fine, too, though in today's multifaceted social network, the more out in the open your "thank you" can be, the better.

A great example of a very simple thank-you status update is this one from Kris and Lindy Boustedt for their film campaign for *This Is Ours*. On Facebook, they thanked a contributor by stating, "Backer 134 is the talented local actress Darlene Sellers. Thank you Darlene!" While this is a fine thank-you, you can, of course, get even more personal and at times pretty creative with your thank-you tweets and updates. For instance, the guys and girls behind the zombie film spoof *Red Scare* kept true to their campaign strategy in their thank-you, maintaining the 1950s-style "Patriotic America" motif and, of course, silly humor: "We all knew she was a real American hero... but now we know she's even Americaner. Hilda Rozas. Thank you."

Also, think of the benefit of thanking someone up close and personally. If you thank contributors directly for all your social networks to see, that will most likely pave the path to further contributions, especially if you're thanking a fair amount of people per day. Plus, this behavior of exercising good manners will also help build up your "social proof" or "social currency," which we'll touch more on a little later. But beware: If other contributors unearth the dark truth that a humble contributor gave even as little as $5 to your campaign and you *didn't* thank them, watch out!

Thank Your Supporters

Not everyone is going to have even $5 to contribute to your crowdfunding campaign, no matter how awesome your film is going to be, or no matter how much they would like to give money to it. People who can't give financially to a campaign tend to support you in other ways, mainly by helping get the word out about your campaign to their friends and followers, some of whom may be able to fork up the money, get a cool perk, and have the honor of saying they're a contributor to this campaign.

So apart from thanking actual contributors, it's equally important to thank any- and everybody who supports your project in other ways. Those who retweet your tweets about your film campaign or share your link on Facebook deserve a little recognition. It's polite and shows them that you appreciate their part in getting the word out about your film campaign. Remember that C-Team we talked about back in Chapter Eight? This is how you build that team up.

Again, here's another prime example of a heartfelt Twitter thank-you from @samplat (Sam Platizky of *Red Scare*):

Another example is a tweet from Leilani Holmes (@moment-soffilm), which reads, "Thanks to everyone who's been RT-ing our Indiegogo campaign for #ClowningAroundFilm. You Rock Our Big Red Noses!" Heartfelt and relevant to the campaign for Damien Cullen's short film *Clowning Around* about two clowns battling to be *the* Bozo of the Big Top.

THE "MAGIC WORD" STILL WORKS MAGIC

While urgency is understandable, especially when crowdfunding in an "All or Nothing" fashion, your tweets and updates, emails, and other forms of online promotion should still employ the word "please" whenever possible, or its popular abbreviations "pls" or "plz." No one wants to feel as though you are demanding a contribution and support. The word "please" softens this determination ever so slightly while demonstrating a certain element of humility in a campaigner, which can go a very long way with crowdfunding.

At one point in your crowdfunding, you may not need to add the "plz RT" anymore, depending on how compelling the wording of your tweets and updates are, and that'll save you some characters, especially on Twitter. But even if you don't have to ask anymore, you should be sure to thank anyone who retweets on your campaign's behalf.

Send Contributors Something Now *and* Later

Ralph Waldo Emerson once wrote, "With the past, I have nothing to do; nor with the future. I live now," and so do the people who contribute to your film campaign. Therefore, you should give them something more immediate than a signed copy of the DVD or Blu-ray when the film's finished several months after your campaign has ended. As I already mentioned, whenever possible this incentive should be personalized for the contributor at one of the lower levels and should be somehow related to your film, like these awesome perks from *Sync*:

I contributed to Brendon's short film, and then received my perks — a pair of records from Brendon's personal collection (he threw in the Idris Muhammad LP because, between that and Sammy Davis Jr., he couldn't decide which to send me) and a pair of *Sync* stickers

18.2. *My* Sync *perks. – a pair of records and a nifty sticker!*

— a couple of weeks after I clicked "Contribute Now" on the Indiegogo. I now had a constant reminder of *Sync* until the film was finished and I was able to watch it when it became available on Vimeo.

Erin Li, one of eight filmmakers selected by the American Film Institute to participate in their Directing Workshop for Women in 2013, ran an Indiegogo for her short science-fiction film *Kepler X-47*, and one of her perks was a digital certificate of existence, which ties in directly to the high concept of the story she was telling through her film about a woman's struggle to adjust to her new life in a human zoo exhibit on an alien planet.

Not only is this kind of incentive innovative and personal, offering contributors a glimpse into Erin's world, but it's also *immediate*. Once it's created, it can be posted to the funder's Facebook wall, tweeted, and/or, in my case, emailed. Again, from there, friends of those funders can post their certificate of existence on their Facebook pages, and their friends can say, "I want a certificate of existence, too!" then visit *Kepler X-47*'s Indiegogo and contribute to the film's existence.

These are the basics of crowdfunder etiquette, which is really about making people feel appreciated by publicly acknowledging them for all the good things they're doing on your behalf. Nothing builds up more *Te* than being a grateful, humble person. And building up integrity is what it takes to not only get through one crowdfunding campaign, but to build a reputation as a fine paradigm of what a crowdfunder *should* be, a person who understands how to treat his or her contributors and supporters, as well as the indie film community as a whole.

• Part Three •
Summary Points

- For a successful film campaign, the "three Ps" of Pitch, Perks, and Promotion are out, and these are now "In" — Invitation, Incentives, and Interactions.

- Your invitation should include an introduction, the invitation itself, the showcase, and a call of action.

- Investors give to projects, people give to people.

- There are three types of incentives you should offer to potential contributors: standard definition, Hi-Def, and 3-D!.

- On social media, focus on interactions before crowdfunding, interactions *and* promotion during your campaign.

- Transparency is a key component in any crowdfunding campaign, so be sure contributors and supporters see all of your behind-the-scenes activities so you can build up their trust.

- Crowdfunder etiquette, or good manners, includes basics like saying "please" and "thank you" and sending your contributors something for the present and the future.

• Part Three •
Exercises

1. Draft an invitation script that includes an *introduction* (who you are), the *invite* itself, which explains what your film is about (*logline*), why you're crowdfunding (*purpose*), and what some of your perks are, and a list of prior work through which you'd like to *showcase* your talent. Then, think about why we should help you make your film, and convince us to act upon it (*call of action*).

2. Take a moment to think about some of your incentives. Which ones can you make all about your potential contributors?

Which one or two could you send to them immediately? Are any of your incentives relevant to your film?

3. What movies are you planning on watching this week? Be sure to tell people about it on social media, and engage in discussions about those films with other like-minded moviegoers. Do you like Stanley Kubrick's movies? Tweet it to the world, and interact with anyone who has something to say about everything from *Fear and Desire* to *Eyes Wide Shut* and everything in between.

PART
4

COMMUNITY
ENGAGEMENT

Chapter Nineteen

• • •

Pu: Let Your Community Help
Carve Your Uncarved Block

EVERYONE'S PROBABLY HEARD the phrase "no one's an island" before, and this is very true with crowdfunding. The same way you should avoid jumping into a film campaign without a proper team or a set strategy, you should avoid thinking you can do this alone. The very nature of crowdfunding dictates otherwise. Without an actual crowd coming together for the common purpose of your project, no money could be raised, and your film would remain on the page, perhaps indefinitely.

Your crowdfunding campaign can be compared to an uncarved block — or *Pu* — that needs to be carved into something. According to Lao Tzu in the *Tao Te Ching*, we are the essence of *Pu* when we are born, and through time and experience, we allow the world to carve us into who and what we are meant to be. The difficulty lies in staying receptive to the natural flow of the world around us. With crowdfunding, your film campaign is the uncarved block, and though we think we as campaigners have full control over the fate of our campaigns and films, that's only partially true. A successful campaign depends not only on its campaigner, but on the community as well.

Indiegogo once had an acronym to describe this: *DIWO*, or *Do It With Others*. I would say that this is the core of crowdfunding — *community engagement*. Just as you might set up a lemonade stand as a child and expect your closest neighbors and members of your immediate family to be among the first to walk over and buy one for a buck, you can expect the same from your immediate online community. This is especially true today. If you have an original product — a local homemade brew of beer, for instance — you will attract the attention of your surrounding community. Because this brew is "local" and "homemade," people will be more likely to give their money to your brand as opposed to picking up another domestic beer like Yuengling that's brewed in the next state over. If your product is well received, that same community may start talking and spread the word about this awesome, local craft beer to others.

This is a very organic means by which to get your project to stretch out across the country, even the world, in an online sense. Just how the local brewer probably doesn't have the finances to physically market his or her beer to bars and lounges all over the US, most DIY filmmakers don't have the means to spread the word about their projects through business cards, printed full-color posters, and other expensive promotional materials, and instead rely on a fully digital form of grassroots word-of-mouth campaigning through their online community. But first you have to build that community and make them care about your particular film.

If you have a must-see film on your hands and are passionate about getting that film into the world, the people in your community *will* come to your aid, sometimes with not only money, but also with their time and other services that may ultimately help you with your campaign and your finished film. Though we may feel that DIY filmmaking is really doing it ourselves, it doesn't have to be. Here's how to make your community care about you, your campaign, and, above all, your film.

• • •

Chapter Twenty

The Golden Rule: "Don't Solicit, Elicit"

Community is a powerful tool when it comes to spreading the word about your crowdfunding campaign on social media. Perhaps the greatest aspect of community is that in most cases it *will* come to bat for you when you need it most. It can be that friend who lends you his or her couch for a month while you're looking for a new apartment, or that trusted professor who'll take time out of his or her day and write up a recommendation letter you need to send to some graduate school the following morning.

As with anything or anyone, you have to know how to make people *want* to help you. More often than not, you may be able to go to a family member or a good friend and ask them for something directly. But what about random people, some of who may be strangers or, at best, friends of friends twice removed by way of the Internet? How do you ask them for a contribution to your film campaign and at the same time make them actually want to contribute?

I find my Twitter feed frequently bombarded by crowdfunding campaigns all vying for attention amidst hundreds of followers. For those of us in the indie film community, this has become a common occurrence. During the first years of the crowdfunding boom, what I found cluttering my feed were repetitious "Help make it happen for" tweets and those punctuated by a "please RT," which asks anyone who reads this tweet to retweet (RT) it to their followers in an attempt to further the campaigner's reach. Now, while there's nothing wrong with tweets of this sort, the draw-backs are that they don't (1) make me want to retweet them; (2)

make me want to check out the campaign; or (3) make me care anything about the project. I might look at the campaign simply because I know the person, but that may not be a good enough reason for most people to help spread the word or contribute.

When you *elicit* help, on the other hand, it makes the community want to support you and spread the word about your project. The prime difference between soliciting and eliciting is that when you solicit something, you simply ask for it head-on, whereas when you elicit something, you're evoking a reaction from another person. It means the difference between this tweet by James Huffman soliciting help for his film *Trails of Gray* about a careworn couple who goes hiking to find closure — "Good morning! Make a donation today for @Trailsofgray. Help make it happen at @Indiegogo" — and this one from Shane Monahan and his film *Musket* eliciting support from the crowd — "Sure, we could've put the script on the shelf, but we believe in #Musket and #indiefilm! Every buck helps!" A little personality will always go the distance.

Here's this difference illustrated in a more practical setting: You see your friend thoroughly enjoying a piece of steak, cooked just the way you like it. It's dripping with juices and smells unbearably delicious. So you *ask* him, "Can I have a piece of your steak?" to which your friend now has the option to say yay or nay. Your friend has the power over you. Now, if you look at that steak and salivate over it — well, that won't work either because that's just sad. But if you look up from that magnificent bit of medium-well goodness and say to your friend something along the lines of, "Man, that steak looks and smells delicious!" as a statement, you will elicit a reaction from your friend, which will most likely be "It is… " (wait for it) "… Do you want to try a piece?" Now *you've* got the power and soon after, a tasty piece of steak.

With regard to crowdfunding, then, and bringing in contributions as well as your community's help, you want to evoke in them the feeling that they *need to* help you and your campaign in some way.

That's where you should get a little creative with your tweets, since eliciting a reaction from people is not an easy task, and to evoke a response that's strong enough to get them to give you money can be even trickier. This is why many crowdfunders I know succumb to the solicitation method — it's much easier to simply ask and in the next minute either see a retweet or not, see a spike in your total funds raised. Or not. (More on this in Chapter Twenty-Eight.)

An acquaintance of mine named Princeton Holt ran an unsuccessful Kickstarter for his feature-length film *The Butterfly Chasers*. Three days before the conclusion of his campaign, he submitted an article he wrote to Film Courage outlining the five things he learned from crowdfunding. One of his "sobering realities" was that "just because you support them, don't assume they will support you," and of course this is true. In terms of contributing funds to a campaign, there are a ton of variables to consider. In terms of other types of support, however, you as the crowdfunder should show people a good enough reason for them to care about your film. If you do, they will feel compelled to support you. Admittedly, this happens to me with very few projects, but when a campaigner compels me to support his or her film campaign, I don't just click the "Retweet" button, I craft my own tweet as a testament to just how much this person had moved me to pitch in.

Filmmaker Lucas McNelly's Kickstarter for *A Year Without Rent* had been stagnant for the long haul of the campaign, yet found success in its final days and hours. This video project was pulled out of the Sarlacc pit of unfunded dreams by the strength of the entire indie film community. This is an exceptional case, of course, but the lesson is standard: *If you show passion for your project and a willingness to drive it forward even in the face of failure, your community will more than likely come to your aid.*

About a year after my crowdfunding campaign for *Cerise* ended and the film was ready for festival submissions, I launched a series of "Crusades for *Cerise*," in which I'd seek film festival submission funds from friends and followers. Whenever I would promote a given Crusade, I made sure each tweet and status update on Facebook was unique and cleverly worded. Sure enough, my followers retweeted it to their followers. I never had to *ask* anyone to "please RT" because I had also built up some credibility by showing them that I take pride not only in my film but also in every minute detail that makes up the whole of *Cerise*, from crowdfunding campaign to production and ultimately to my Crusades.

Another way to elicit a boost to the awareness factor of your film campaign on social media is to try to land some interviews and spots on various Internet radio shows. Plenty of filmmakers and indie film enthusiasts run shows on Blog Talk Radio like *Rex Sikes' Movie Beat* and *Cutting Room Floor* with Casey Ryan. If you're doing a good job with your campaigning and standing out amidst the flood of crowdfunding campaigns rushing down your Twitter and Facebook feeds, you may nab the attention of influencers like these, just like I did, and that can spread your crowdfunding campaign to an even wider audience, and maybe even attract the attention of some major players and payers as well.

The more you practice the art of elicitation, the easier it will become to bring together a community invested in the welfare of your film, and the more instrumental they will be in helping you carve out a successful campaign and leading you toward a crowdfunding success. With all the crowdfunding traffic circulating in the vastness of the Internet, you *must* stand out not only with your film's logline and campaign strategy, but also with each and every interaction you have. People forget things; if they see you're reaching out for a retweet and you give them the chance to think to themselves, *I'll retweet this later*, chances are they won't. Your outreach should therefore be compelling enough to make the person stop whatever he or she is doing and lend a helping hand to you and your campaign immediately.

Chapter Twenty-One

* * *

THE IMPORTANCE OF KEEPING YOUR CONTRIBUTORS UPDATED

Matthew Broderick says it best in *Ferris Bueller's Day Off:* "Life moves pretty fast. If you don't stop and look around once in a while, you could miss it." That was back in 1986. Today, the world moves inconceivably fast, and this is especially true for the entertainment industry, indie or otherwise. The advent of social media has even made information flow at real-time speeds. Many of us do our best to keep up with this rushing tide and at the same time try to create our own fresh content so we have something meaningful to share with the world.

Keeping people updated about your film campaign is integral to the lifespan of your crowdfunding efforts. This is especially true with regard to your contributors, since they have some stake in seeing how the film turns out. Whether they're actual investors or everyday Joes and Janes giving money for particular perks, most contributors don't give money and then forget about your film campaign. They want to see what is released into the world once it's complete, so keep them updated about every aspect of your project, from crowdfunding to film festival screenings.

There are many ways to do this, and with so many variables, we can quickly become overwhelmed. Questions will pile up: How many emails are too many? What's the right number of social media sites to keep active on? When should I set up my film's website? These are just a few of the topics that, when fixated on, can hinder a successful campaign, so I've included some principal methods of keeping your contributors, followers, and friends updated with the goings-on of your crowdfunding campaign.

EMAIL UPDATES: TRIED AND TESTED

At one point during my crowdfunding seminar at Golden Door International Film Festival of Jersey City, my cohost Slava Rubin posed a question to the audience: "Which method brings in the most money — email, Facebook, or Twitter?" The majority of the audience (myself included at the time) said Twitter. Some others raised their hands in praise of Facebook. Practically no one chose the correct answer, which is email. We've gotten so hung up on social media that we sometimes forget that email is really the progenitor of all modern modes of communication.

You should send your contributors updates via email at least once a week during your campaigning. With *Cerise*, I sent out occasional emails to my modest network, keeping them in the know about how close I was getting to my $5,000 target. Many of them would see that last week the number was at $2,350 and today it had jumped to $2,700. When your network sees that people are supporting your film financially, they may be more likely to put in $5 or $10 since "everyone else is doing it."

This is all about building up your *social proof*, your value as perceived through the eyes of your community via social media and, in this case, crowdfunding. According to Indiegogo, once a campaign reaches 30% of its crowdfunding goal, that's when random people will start contributing to the campaign. By random people, I don't mean your close friends on your contact list, since they should be among the first to contribute. I mean those who are more professional contacts, the ones you don't lunch with on a weekly basis, and even complete strangers. Show them that others are doing it, and they will do it too.

UPDATES ACROSS SOCIAL MEDIA

As easy as it may be to update your Facebook status and send out a tweet, people who are new to social media will realize that there are a ton of sites out there, some for everyday interactions like Facebook and Twitter, others tailored to more general and professional contact like LinkedIn, and many that are specified for the film and entertainment industry, like Stage 32. Then there's Digg, Reddit, StumbleUpon, Path, Pinterest, Tumblr — the list goes on and on and on further still.

The ultimate question is this: How can I possibly keep my contributors updated on *all* of these social networking websites? The answer is simple: You can't. I attended a panel about social media and filmmaking, and one of the panelists, Leslie Poston, author of *Social Media Metrics for Dummies*, coauthor of *Twitter for Dummies*, and head of digital and social at McKinsey & Company, said that a person should be active on no more than five social media sites in order to maximize one's content output. Coming from someone who is well over 70,000 tweets strong, I'd put my money on that answer.

Once you've chosen your five social networks, you can then friend or follow your contributors and keep them updated a bit more than once a week. I told contributors in an early email that if they want monthly updates, they should visit *Cerise's* website or subscribe to its RSS feed; if they want more frequent updates, they should add me as a friend on Facebook (we didn't have a Facebook page for *Cerise* just yet); if they want real-time updates, Twitter's the way to go. By wording it this way, you give your contributors a choice of how they'd like to be updated about your film and campaign, which makes it about them.

You might also want to consider creating a separate Twitter handle for your film like @TiltheMovie and @AroundHereFilm did, if separation of filmmaker from film is something that's important to you. But again, by doing this, you add more to your plate when the very essence of *Pu* is simplicity. Therefore, keep it simple. I didn't feel the need to create @CeriseMovie for Twitter because for a time that was the only interesting thing I was tweeting about as @Trigonis, so *Cerise* became synonymous with my personal Twitter handle. And since personalization is what this kind of campaigning is about, it was a fine fit for *Cerise* and others like it and may be for your film campaign as well.

WEBSITES, BLOGS, AND OTHER WAYS TO UPDATE

Now you're ready to move into the big time. Eventually, your film, whether still in the crowdfunding stages or packaged and ready for film festival submissions, will need a website that offers basic information: a synopsis, director's statement, cast and crew list, some production stills, and a trailer. On most websites, there's a "News" section as well, which is good for updates about all that's happening with your film for people discovering your movie for the first time.

Years ago, setting up a website was an incredibly expensive endeavor. Add to that the cost of a Webmaster to maintain your site and keep it updated. Today, there are new DIY ways to keep costs low so you don't need a separate crowdfunding campaign for website funds. Many indie filmmakers customize a standard blog site like Wordpress or Tumblr. By going this route, you get a functional website with free hosting. The website for *Cerise* is nothing more than a modified Wordpress page.

There are also websites like Squarespace and Wix, which offer more professional customizable features for a relatively low monthly cost that won't break the bank. Splashy Flash pages with animated graphics should be reserved for Hollywood movies. A website for an indie short or feature-length film should be informational at the very least, which means a blog will work wonders.

21.1. *For Cerise's website, I used a customized Wordpress. For a short film, a blog site works perfectly fine.*

For added pizzazz, many of these blog sites allow you to upload your own background photos and designs to further appeal to people visiting your page for the first time. For further options for customization, however, you may be required to move from the freemium to the premium tier. All in all, it will still be much less expensive than hiring a Webmaster to create and update a more traditional website.

NOW THAT IT'S OVER...

Even after you've crowdfunded like a rock star, thanked all your contributors, and mailed away their perks, you're only just beginning to *see* the finish line. The same way it's important to keep your contributors updated throughout your campaign, it's just as important to maintain a steady flow of updates about the progress of your film after the campaign has ended. Your contributors have funded your film for various reasons, so the least you should do is make them feel like they're a part of something bigger than themselves because to many of them, helping to fund a film is kind of a big deal.

Perhaps *Cerise* funder Andrew Bichler says it best in a short video about why he contributed to my short film: "What really turned me on [was] the fact that I, as an everyday guy, could get involved in funding and supporting the arts..." You heard it right from a proud backer's mouth. As such, it's gratifying to be kept in the loop about what's going on regarding a film you've become an integral part of. I receive regular updates with behind-the-scenes footage, postproduction notes, and other status updates from many of the nearly 100 film campaigns I've contributed to, like *What Lola Wants*, *Around Here*, and *Iron Sky: The Coming Race*. If you don't update your audience, they may start to think all kinds of outrageous things, the worst of which quite possibly being, *Well, I won't support that person's campaigns anymore!*

Again, it's all about appreciation, so you should treat your contributors with the same high level of respect you might show an investor whether he or she has contributed at the $1 rung or higher up toward the top of the crowdfunding ladder.

Chapter Twenty-Two

• • •

AVOIDING "THE FLOOD"

WHEN COMPANIES ATTEMPT to engage their customers too frequently or too forcefully, it ultimately leads to disengagement. Taoism is all about balance. When crowdfunding and promoting your film, you need to maintain a solid line between getting word out about your campaign to potential contributors and being a pest. With crowdfunding, it should also be mentioned that you are approaching people who haven't signed up for it. Therefore, if you cross that line, your contacts may be less likely to trust you than they might a tried and tested clothing company like Old Navy.

Even though every drop in a body of water is unique, when viewed collectively in large volume, that singularity disappears and we're left with just water. The same holds true for the following two ways that are certain to flood away your supporters.

EMAIL INUNDATION

As mentioned in the previous chapter, email can be a great tool for both promoting your crowdfunding campaign and keeping your contributors and email contacts and backers updated. As with anything, though, too much is too much, and you should find a balance and strive to keep it. This doesn't necessarily mean you should only send out an email zealously on the second Tuesday of every month. That's not balance, either, because what if something extraordinary happens in the interim? In today's e-world, "yesterday's news is tomorrow's fish and chip paper," to borrow a line from an Elvis Costello song. When something happens this morning, it's old news by the afternoon.

Emails should therefore be sent out strategically and never, never once a day (the email "blast" is the past, so let's keep it where it belongs), since even that can be construed by most as a nuisance, and you will get the inevitable email that all crowdfunders dread: "Please unsubscribe me from this email, thank you." And, of course, not every email will be this kindly worded.

SOCIAL DELUGE

Flooding your social media feed with the same material can oftentimes lead to unfollowing on Twitter, unfriending on Facebook, and unpleasantries all around. I see this at times from crowdfunders, as well as some of the more hardcore supporters of crowdfunding, many of whom can't contribute to a given film campaign so they overcompensate by boosting their level of social media support to the status of "annoying."

On the following page is an example of this type of constant tweeting from Antony D. Lane (@IndywoodFILMS), who at the time had been crowdfunding his feature-length film *Invasion of the Not Quite Dead* since May of 2009, campaigning 24/7 (almost literally!) and independent of any crowdfunding platform.

While this isn't such a terrible thing for crowdfunders themselves, it can be quite a hassle to scroll through if you have friends who only go on Facebook to see what their friends are doing. It may be annoying for them to speed past an abundance of updates and Indiegogo or Kickstarter links. It can be (and has been) grounds for unfriending and unfollowing, truth be told. Therefore, you should keep aware of how many times per day you promote your campaign and, of course, keep a balance between your personal and your crowdfunding lives.

22.1. *An example of @IndywoodFILM's nonstop tweeting for his feature-length film*
Invasion of the Not Quite Dead.

DAM IT!

But let's be realistic: Crowdfunding means marketing. So how can
we find this much-needed balance I keep talking about? With
regard to email outreach, you can set up a separate account for
your film via your website or create a separate email account and
import your contacts. The one thing you'll have to be sure to do,
of course, is to mention this in your first email from that account

so that people don't automatically put a block on an email from an unknown source. Also, people can opt out early on in case they're not interested in your crowdfunding campaign but still would like to keep you as their contact.

A simple fix for your social flooding problems is to designate different social networking sites for different purposes. For instance, Instagram is a photo-sharing platform that doesn't allow users to post links within each post. That said, save the links to your campaign for Facebook, and use Instagram to share photos of your incentives or other visual content related to your campaign.

Of all the social networking sites, Twitter is probably the best hybrid for both business and personal interaction with your following, so you shouldn't run into any issues posting personal thoughts and opinions as well as promotional information about your crowdfunding campaign. You may choose to only promote your film's campaign on Twitter, which appears to be a solid idea, looking at Lane's campaign as a prime example. As of May 2012, he had a massive following of over 101,000 people watching and waiting to see how "the world's first 100% Twitter fan funded horror film trilogy" turns out when it's all over. That number has since risen to 182,000, on top of a 21,000-person-strong fan base on the film's own Twitter account (@IOTNQDmovie).

Charlie Chaplin says it best in his famous speech at the end of *The Great Dictator*: "You are not machines… you are men!" (And women!) That said, you should not flood your feed with tweets and updates exclusively about your campaign, no matter how creatively worded they may be. The objects of marketing in crowdfunding are to raise funds, build a community comprised of contributors and supporters to help make your campaign stronger, and intricately carve out of that *Pu* a masterpiece of a campaign — and not disfigure it with quantity lacking quality.

...

Chapter Twenty-Three

"I'VE GOT NO MONEY, BUT I *CAN* GIVE _____!"

HERE'S A FACT that crowdfunders don't like to admit: Sometimes people really don't have any money to give to a film campaign. But there's so much more to crowdfunding than raising money and awareness. There's also the *crowdsourcing* element that sometimes gets lost in crowdfunding. In a nutshell, crowdsourcing means reaching out to the crowd to obtain anything at all, not only the money you need to make your film. Crowdfunding can be about obtaining other things just as valuable, if not more so, than funding and free promotion.

Perhaps my good friend and former Indiegogo colleague Adam Chapnick says it best: "If you're crowdfunding for the money, you're doing it wrong." Even when I first heard this, I was confused. That's the very nature of crowd*funding*, right? Wrong. The very nature of *crowd*funding is the crowd. And we never know who might make up our particular crowd. For instance, because of his success crowdfunding *A Year Without Rent* on Kickstarter, Lucas McNelly attracted the attention of the entire indie film community, and thus became a collaborator on various other projects thanks to the very nature of *A Year Without Rent*. To be a filmmaker, you don't make just one film, you make *films*, so the more help you can attract, the more films you'll make.

Aside from collaborators on future film projects, filmmakers have also received press opportunities because of their crowdfunding campaigns. Sometimes, and especially if you're keeping a solid connection with prominent social media influencers, you can attract the attention of those bloggers, websites like Indiewire, and Internet radio programs like *Cutting Room Floor* and *Rex Sikes' Movie Beat*, which I mentioned in a previous chapter. This kind of press can substantially boost awareness about your crowdfunding campaign and build up your credibility as well. A one-hour spot on the popular LA Talk Radio program *Film Courage* should be treated like a ten-minute spot on *The Late Show with Stephen Colbert*.

Another prime example is film producer Sarah Marder, who received some really outstanding press in one of the country's most prestigious magazines — *The Atlantic* — for her documentary *The Genius of a Place*, which explores the intricate differences between an agrarian-based economy and one that can only thrive through tourism and commercialization. Aside from this notable feat of press, Sarah and her *Genius of a Place*, which surpassed its goal of $20,000 for finishing funds on Indiegogo, was also the subject of Episode 56 of the podcast *Eye on Italy*, since Sarah's documentary is centered in the small town of Cortona, Italy.

Whether it's big or small press, it's *all* press, and because of the Internet, any press has the ability to reach out further than it ever has before. The fact is you never know who's watching. Take Julie Keck and Jessica King, who penned the screenplay for the indie thriller and crowdfunding success story *Tilt*. Aside from being authorities on the subject of social media, the screenwriting duo known throughout the indie film community as King is a Fink are always working on a plethora of projects: Jessica cowrote the narration for a documentary called *A Second Knock at the Door* with *Tilt* backer and director Chris Grimes while Julie handled the social media outreach, and now they are working together on another project for Chris' company 5414 Productions. They also wrote a live game show called *Who Knows Her Better* and a play/web series called *I Hate Tommy Finch*, both for Tello Films — they were introduced to Tello cofounder Christin Mell by another *Tilt* backer. Plus, the girls are working on two feature-length screenplays. All of this came about because people were paying attention to the *Tilt* campaign and saw the innovative things that Julie and Jessica were contributing to it, namely *Tilt* the Town.

Cerise was also on the receiving end of much kindness from one-time strangers who have now become close friends and supporters. Music has always been one of the more difficult things for me as a filmmaker to come by; it was especially difficult before the days of crowdfunding when all of my expenses were out-of-pocket and these pockets didn't run very deep. At one point during my campaign, I was messaging people on Facebook trying to elicit contributions. At the time, I didn't realize the silliness of messaging an indie rock band for a monetary handout — bands are basically pooling their money together to keep them rocking and rolling with their music. So when Kevin Adkins, lead singer/songwriter of Icewagon Flu and Franklin Gotham, actually got in touch with me, I didn't know what to expect. He wrote that he and the band had no money to give, but he then asked if they could donate a song to *Cerise*. Immediately I responded with an emphatic "Yes! That would be awesome."

Icewagon Flu, whose song "Liza Was Rejected" was featured in my prior short film *Perfekt*, wrote up a song called "Cerise," which incorporates all the themes and ideas I explore in the film. The music itself is quirky and fun, and I couldn't have been happier. And during the Big Apple preview of *Cerise*, Icewagon Flu made a guest appearance and played a short acoustic set of their songs, including "Cerise," right before we screened the film for an audience of over 100 friends, family members, and Indiegogo backers.

Not only was I able to get an awesome, catchy title track for *Cerise*, but a few weeks after Icewagon Flu agreed to donate the song, a music composer from Serbia named Nino Rajacic reached out to me and asked if he could donate an entire score to the film. He had discovered my film on Indiegogo and said it sounded like a really cool concept — and something he'd like to have in his credits. Without hesitation, we got to work a few weeks later sharing our ideas, and then Nino sat down and started composing the music. A few minor tweaks later, and *Cerise* had a wonderful score and Nino had some more cinematic music added to his resume. It was a win-win, and all because of crowdfunding.

Cerise also got its website from a backer named Ben Gerber, who initially contributed a substantial amount of money to the film's Indiegogo campaign. Then he asked Marinell and me if we were thinking of setting up a website, and when we told him we were, he brought his brother into the mix to work on designing one from a Wordpress page. Once the website was up and running, Ben surprised us again a couple of weeks later with a domain name, and since then, he has also taken care of the web hosting fees so we can keep *www.cerisemovie.com* up and running all year round.

Funding may be the primary reason we filmmakers launch crowd-funding campaigns, but it shouldn't be the sole reason, because it's only one part of the ongoing battle that is DIY filmmaking. There are so many other variables to take into consideration — from music to marketing, distribution, and beyond — all of which would normally require time and money. However, you never know when someone like Nino may stumble onto your campaign because of a Google search and contribute his editing or sound design skills pro bono because it seems like a worthwhile project. And if you create a strong enough buzz about your film campaign, you'll no doubt attract the attention of film websites and other influencers, the way Lucas and Sarah had done, or find future collaborators to work with like King is a Fink and many others have done, and continue paving the road toward a successful career as a working filmmaker.

. . .

Chapter Twenty-Four

DON'T PANIC! —
HANDLING THE LULL
BETWEEN CONTRIBUTIONS

IT'S BOUND TO happen at least once in every crowdfunding campaign, no matter how expertly crafted and strategized it is. For a time you'll be on a roll, raking in contribution upon contribution. The communities you've reached out to will seem to be coming together in aid of your film campaign, sending out feelers amongst their own various networks and bringing in further funding. Everything will be going smoothly. Maybe a little *too* smoothly. Or maybe just as planned.

And then, without warning, it'll stop.

You may find yourself sitting in front of your computer, smartphone, or tablet refreshing your campaign's homepage only to verify an inconceivable truth: You're stuck at the same dollar amount, and you've been stuck at this same dollar amount for a few hours now. Perhaps even a few days. For many of us, this can be disheartening and might even convince some filmmakers to give up on crowdfunding entirely. I've seen it happen a few times. I've watched campaigns sit through what I call "The Lull" (or what others call "The Dip" and sometimes "The Trough of Despair") like someone caught in a pit of quicksand. Some panic and sink faster while others simply allow themselves to founder until the days count down to zero.

The same thing happened when I was crowdfunding *Cerise*, and it happened very early on in the campaign. I received a few contributions, fulfilled a few digital perks, and then, without warning, an entire day went by without a single contribution. I waited. Then the next day I met with more of the same: Not one backer stepped forward. Not a single retweet on Twitter. Not one reply to my last couple of emails, not even to ask to be removed. So I did what anyone else in this predicament would do. I panicked too.

This was a premature reaction, of course. Shortly after, I realized that there's no sense in panicking since it's completely unproductive. I needed a proactive way to deal with this two-day lull, and that's when I became a lot more playful with my online interactions. I hadn't realized it, but I was putting out the same kind of promotion that companies would do to market a product. But crowdfunding an indie film is not about selling products, it's about movies and the people who make them, and you should have as much fun with your fundraising as you would making your film. So I started reaching out and giving my friends and followers a more personal reason to help *Cerise* as contributors or supporters.

Yes, even something like a lull becomes a question of community engagement. Let's go back to the example of that person stuck in the quicksand. In every movie you can probably think of, it always takes another person to come to the aid of the one who's sinking. That person cannot get out of that predicament by him- or herself. In the case of crowdfunding, amidst a vast desert of campaigns all raising money for various films, it's up to you to show the community why *your* film is worth their support and a little help out from the quicksand.

But you also have to show them that you're not giving up just because a couple of days have passed and none of your followers have seen a "thank-you" tweet or status update welcoming a new contributor into the fold of your film campaign. You have to keep the flow of your campaign moving forward, and oftentimes that means changing your approach to it. This hearkens back to the simple genius of Bruce Lee: "Be water" and you'll flow forward. A few rocks in the path of a stream don't stop the stream. The water will find a way around the rocks, slip between the cracks, and keep moving toward its destination.

In the event of a lull, be creative and innovative, offer some new perks, and try some new things that might wake that lull with the kind of interactions that reengage your community. These innovations may not always work, but they will keep the flow of your campaign constant and on the minds of potential contributors and other supporters. During the lull that *Cerise* endured, Marinell and I brainstormed ways to keep our community engaged. We came up with a few interactive ideas, one of which was a "Spelling Twee," a Twitter-based spelling bee in which we'd tweet an audio link of a word and our followers could then attempt to spell the word out in a tweet. It kept a few people engaged in between my newly personalized promotion tactics, but did not have the success we thought it might.

Another way to stream your way around the rocks of the lull is to run a referral-based contest, in which you award a special perk to a person who brings in the most funding by referring your campaign to their friends and followers. That's sort of what I did with the Spelling Twee. Assuming that the same followers would be playing, whoever got the most words correct would receive a cerise-colored Twibbon, a ribbon that you can append to your Twitter avatar to show support for something. Why a Twibbon? It was pretty trendy at the time, and it's always good to keep up with the latest Twitter trends.

Special incentives are another great way to draw more support from your community, especially if it's "for a limited time only." It shows your community that you're going the extra mile to bring in new contributors and get closer to your fundraising goal.

With *Cerise*, I didn't need to offer any special incentives during its Indiegogo campaign, but during my Third Crusade for *Cerise*, to rack up the submission fees for some of the final festivals I hoped would accept my film, I offered for a limited time a signed DVD of *Cerise*. And that proved incentive enough to get the last few submission fees covered.

The more fun, innovative, and relevant you make your special incentives, however, the faster you'll free your campaign from the lull. A prime example is Gary King's second Kickstarter for his movie musical *How Do You Write a Joe Schermann Song*. This campaign was all about the music — the main reason for it was to raise $18,000 so that Gary could record a score with a live orchestra. His special incentive at any dollar amount was for the backer to give him a word that he would compile for composer Joe Schermann, who would then work it into the lyrics of a song that he'd compose and the cast of *How Do You Write a Joe Schermann Song* would perform. There are about 150 words on this list — 150 backers out of 244 total backers by the end of this second successful campaign.

Although the lull can seem like a frightening place and maybe even make you feel that crowdfunding isn't for you, it's really just a stepping-stone that can help you think more creatively about your campaign. It may even help you discover new, more innovative ways to go about keeping your community invested enough in your film to help you pull your campaign through the dark times and onto the sunlit path ahead.

Chapter Twenty-Five

...

THE FINE ART OF CONSECUTIVE CAMPAIGNING

IF YOU'RE LIKE me, you probably come up with a new logline or ten every day for a film or web series that you feel is a stroke of genius and would make for a lucrative project. Then, after about a week of brushing away all the loglines that couldn't spread their wings and become whole synopses, you may be left with two or three really great ideas that might be worth pursuing. And you want to crowdfund them all, which lots of filmmakers have done already, from Jeanie Finlay (*Sound It Out, Orion: The Man Who Would Be King*) to Timo Vuorensola (*Iron Sky: The Coming Race*).

If you've got the time, the network, a few big spenders, and a strong support system for your prior work, you may be able to run consecutive campaigns like Mattson Tomlin did for his films. Mattson started out with a Kickstarter called "Bring *Solomon Grundy* to Life" in January of 2010 and raised $12,064 of his initial $10,000 goal. A mere five months after that campaign ended, he launched a second one for another short film called *Dream Lover* and exceeded that Kickstarter goal of $8,422 by $6.

While it appears that consecutive campaigning can lead to success, it doesn't hurt to briefly examine the *level* of success. Mattson raised a substantial amount over his goal for his *Solomon Grundy* campaign. However, during his second campaign, he reached his goal, but barely made it a few dollars over the hump — again, *Dream Lover* brought in an additional $6. One can't help wonder what a third campaign might have yielded. Well, after his *Demon Lover* Kickstarter, Mattson ran another campaign for his next film,

Rene, which launched with a excessively lofty goal of $75,000; 151 backers pledged $11,285 to this third campaign from a very talented filmmaker, and one who is active on social media, primarily Twitter, but not active enough to engage the same audience a third time for full funding for *Rene*.

Now, you may have a single story that you're so very passionate about, but it will cost you a lot more than what you think you can raise in a single sitting. With this one film, you can always choose to raise funds in phases, which is another form of consecutive crowdfunding. Simon Cox has been crowdfunding consecutively since 2013 for his science fiction adventure film *Kaleidoscope Man*. His first Kickstarter garnered £2,200 over his goal of £5,000. He came over to Indiegogo because he needed some additional funding, so he set up his campaign for Phase 2, which earned £5,025 on a £5,000 goal. By Phase 3's campaign, perhaps a touch of pride may have gotten the better of Simon when he set a goal at £25,000, which led to his first unsuccessful campaign, raising only £7,082. Trying again in Phase 4 for £20,000, he yet again took home (thanks to Indiegogo's flexible funding model) less than that amount (£6,719). By the time Simon launched Phases 5 and 7 (Phase 6 was bypassed by some outside investment funding), he'd set more modest goals and raised £11,543 and counting.

Kaleidoscope Man certainly had some ups and downs, but let's look at a more important set of numbers, shall we? Phase 1 raised its funds from 186 backers; Phase 2: 105 backers, drop-off most likely due to the transition from Kickstarter to Indiegogo; Phase 3: 165 backers; Phase 4: 231 backers; Phase 5: 208. These are some impressive numbers, because it tells us that through Simon's multiple campaigns for his *Star Wars*–inspired epic he has grown his audience substantially. And yes, by Phase 5 and 7, there was some drop-off, but not much. (Yes, the struggle of *campaign fatigue*, or oversaturation, is quite real.)

Then there's a film like Gary King's *How Do You Write a Joe Schermann Song*, which raised a grand total of $49,132 between two campaigns. We'll discover more of how Gary was able to raise this amount between two campaigns in my crowd study "How Do You Direct [A Gary King Musical] — Build Your Brand," but Gary ran a third campaign for his horror film *Unnerved*, which earned him $13,337 from 262 backers on a $10,000 goal.

The question becomes *how do we as filmmakers crowdfund our films and raise more funds and build our communities further?* Here are some tips to assure the best possible experience with consecutive campaigning for different films or funding one in phases.

BREAK IT UP

After a couple of weeks to a couple of months of crowdfunding, you'll want to take a break before your next one, not just for you, but also for your community and backers. Most people have no qualms about supporting a film to give the filmmaker a chance at the big time. If, however, you want them to contribute again, it may behoove you as a crowdfunder to wait a while, perhaps even until you have some proof that your next film will be as much of a winner as the first film their contributions helped make happen.

You want to gradually work your friends, followers, and supporters into the whole idea that you'll be back, but you don't want to overwork them, either. Crowdfunding is like exercising a muscle. If you push it too hard, you'll be sore the next morning, or worse, you might pull something and possibly do more severe damage.

FULFILLMENT FIRST

This one's huge. If you've run a campaign before, you owe it to all of your contributors to fulfill as many of those incentives as possible before embarking on another campaign for the same or another film. I've contributed to a lot of campaigns, and I always check back to see what those crowdfunding filmmakers are up to, and when I see that they've launched a new campaign but I'm still waiting on my T-shirt or personalized thank-you video, I feel a little cheated.

I do know that before I saw the Indiegogo for *Kaleidoscope Man*, Phase 4, my perk for Phase 3 was at my doorstep from across the pond. The thing to keep in mind is you're most likely going to be drawing from the same pool of people, and if you don't fulfill what they already paid for before expecting them to give again to another campaign, they won't contribute to that campaign.

KEEP CONNECTED

While you're taking that break in between your first and next indie film campaigns, you'll want to keep your backers, followers, and the indie film community engaged on all the social media channels you've built up before and during your campaign. If you stop interacting with people, they may start wondering what happened to you.

Allowing your community to carve out the *Pu* of your indie film (and perhaps your career as an indie filmmaker) doesn't take a break; it's constant, and it's on *you* as filmmaker to keep it constant by consistently growing your following. Are you putting enough value into the social mediascape? Are you meeting new people in person at local events? In short, what you are doing to earn more friends, followers, and contacts dictates what role they will play in helping you fund your subsequent films down the line.

Through his seven campaigns for *Kaleidoscope Man*, Simon was able to raise over £37,000 to shoot most of the movie, including a scene with a tank! He may not have had the network to do this in one shot back in 2013, but by the end, that audience grew, and in order to get the funding we need, we've gotta have a crowd that wants to help out. Then, finding himself with no time to do a campaign for an eighth phase, Simon reached out to the audience he'd been keeping updated this whole time for funds to shoot the final scenes of the *Kaleidoscope Man* on the island of Lanzarote, and thirteen people came to his aid to help him with the last bit of funding he needed to shoot these alien planet scenes.

TURN SELF-CONFIDENCE INTO SELF-AWARENESS

"Hubris" is the ancient Greek word for excessive pride or self-confidence. Many of us probably first learned about hubris from Sophocles' play *Oedipus the King* or Aristotle's *Poetics*, in which he cites this particular play as the greatest ever written and spends the bulk of the book explaining why. For those uninitiated, part one of the Oedipus Cycle tells the story of a Theban king who couldn't accept the fact that he had killed his father and married his mother because of his own pride until it's too late, and he physically blinds himself because of the mental blindness he suffers from as his tragic flaw.

From a crowdfunding perspective, hubris translates to having what Han Solo calls delusions of grandeur, which manifests itself in different ways. Most common, however, is setting an extremely high goal disproportionate to the previous goal(s) you've set. Mattson ran two successful campaigns, one with a goal of $10,000, the other with a goal of $8,422, and then jumped his goal for *Rene* up to $75,000; Simon ran two successful campaigns with goals set modestly at £5,000 each. He increased his third goal by 400%, but his audience, though substantially grown, wasn't quite at the level where they would get him to £25,000. Not yet, anyway. The same goes for Mattson and countless others. We've got to work our way up to that level of social currency so we can one day cash it in for the bigger bucks we need to make those bigger films better.

The truth is we *all* suffer from a little hubris at one point or another; it's simply what we call self-confidence. It's when things don't go quite the way we want them to that we become aware. And while self-confidence is not necessarily a tragic flaw, *self-awareness* is the greatest strength. Therefore, it's important for us to check ourselves and put into perspective what we realistically can and cannot accomplish with crowdfunding. Then we'll always find the right level of success.

Chapter Twenty-Six

• • •

BUILD RELATIONSHIPS, NOT TRANSACTIONS

SLAVA RUBIN SAYS it best: "The world is shifting from a world of transactions to a world of relationships." Nowadays, no one wants to be treated like a customer, and I don't think anyone ever did before. When it comes to crowdfunding for your film, everything you are putting into your campaign — time, money, marketing, and every interaction — should be grounded firmly in the idea of building relationships as opposed to networks or connections. Not every contributor will be an actual investor in your film project, giving a large sum of money and hoping for a return on their investment, plus a little extra. Some of them will be everyday people giving to your campaign in exchange for a specific perk or reward. Both kinds of contributors are key to the future of your film. Therefore, it's important to always give them more, to strive to make them feel more special than just another customer, and there are a few ways to do this.

SUPPORT IS A TWO-WAY STREET

One way is to treat your contributors the same way you would treat your actual friends, both online and offline. If certain contributors are fellow filmmakers or other kinds of artists, an easy way to make them feel like they're more than just a person who gave you funding for your film is to support them in their own artistic endeavors. That means if they have a film screening happening in your area, make an effort to attend. If they're musicians and are about to release a new album, be one of the first to buy or download it, and then write a review about it. It's important to take time and reciprocate in some way the support that other artists have shown you during your crowdfunding campaign.

PROMOTE YOURSELF *AND* OTHERS?

When I was crowdfunding *Cerise*, I was online all day long except when I had to sleep, and even that was at a minimum. Everyone knew that I was crowdfunding for my short film, and many of my first backers weren't family members or friends, but other film-makers, a few of whom were crowdfunding their own films at the same time. This confused me at first, my initial thought being *why are these friends and followers contributing to my short film when they're trying to raise money for their own films?* It would make much more sense to put one's own money into his or her own campaign and not give $25 to this campaign and $10 to that, since that's $35 that could help bump their campaign's total closer toward its crowdfunding goal.

After some thought, it became very clear to me that this indie film community I had gotten involved with was indeed a community in the truest sense, and this was just another way of interacting with that community. Everyone was there to help everyone else one way or another. Many times, this meant contributing to *Cerise*, but those who couldn't contribute financially to my campaign helped out by spreading the word about *Cerise* to their networks, and from some of those referrals financial support flowed in. When something as organic as this happens, you should pay back the people responsible for it, and one way to do this is with a contribution or spreading the word about their projects to your network. Yin and yang in perfect non-action! (But more on that in the next part of this book.)

Haters Gonna Hate (But Filmmakers Gonna Make)

There are, however, people who will not necessarily share these sentiments and only be in it for themselves. They may *not* help you back if you help push them on by showing encouragement for their projects. They might *not* necessarily contribute to your campaign even though you poured fifty of your hard-earned dollars into their campaign instead of your own. It's unfortunate, but these people do exist, and you will encounter them. The worst thing you can do is succumb to these unpromising circumstances and allow the bad taste to remain in your mouth. One rotten apple does not spoil the bunch. Toss it out and keep on keeping on.

We all know that people have a tendency to judge others by the company they keep. In that sense, we should heed the advice of the ancient Greek philosopher Epictetus, who tells us "the key is to keep company only with people who uplift you, whose presence calls forth your best." That is also the secret message of *Pu*, the uncarved block. It requires us to let our world and those who come into contact with it mold us into only our very best, much the way our contributors will mold the success of our campaigns by giving money, support, a score, a website — anything at all that will enhance our crowdfunding efforts. All of it will ultimately make our finished films the best they can be.

"When the block is carved, it becomes useful," says Lao Tzu in his *Tao Te Ching*. In that sense, those who help us carve it are responsible for so much more than any simple professional network can bestow. They are friends in the truest sense of the word.

• PART FOUR •
SUMMARY POINTS

- Don't solicit (ask). Elicit (evoke).

- Promote strongly through email and on social media, but avoid email inundation and social deluge ("The Flood") at all costs.

- With crowdfunding, support can come in various forms, from financial contributions and investment to donations of music scores, websites, and the many other costly aspects of movie-making that turn a good film into a great one.

- "The Lull" should be seen as an opportunity to switch up your campaign strategy as opposed to a white flag signaling surrender.

- Build a relationship with every dollar raised; in doing so, you avoid the pitfall of treating contributors and supporters as nothing more than transactions.

• PART FOUR •
EXERCISES

1. A little practice in the art of elicitation versus the act of solicitation: Come up with five different ways to write "Please help support this crowdfunding campaign for my film." How might you make people *want* to contribute?

2. Think about your film and its many components, from cinematography to scoring and distribution. What three things would you most like to obtain other than funding for your film?

3. Let's pretend you've hit a lull, perhaps even before your campaign has started to really pick up steam. It may be your invitation — the teaser for your film, or the fact that your best incentive is also your most expensive. Maybe you're flooding your network with more promotion than interaction. How would you not only fix these issues, but also improve upon the standard solutions?

PART 5

THE *TAO* OF
SOCIAL MEDIA

...

Chapter Twenty-Seven

WEI WU WEI:
"DOING WITHOUT (OVER)DOING"

IN VERSE THIRTY-SEVEN of the *Tao Te Ching*, Lao Tzu describes one of the most important principles of Taoism, which is also one of the more difficult to attain, let alone fully understand: "Tao abides in non-action," he begins, "Yet nothing is left undone. / If kings and lords observed this, / The ten thousand things would develop naturally." This is *wu wei* — the principle of "non-action."

Today, this concept of non-action is even more difficult for many people to fathom. How can anyone get anything done without making an effort to get it done? Without planning ahead? Without strategy or desire? In a crowdfunding sense, there's absolutely no way that your "ten thousand" dollars would be raised if we "kings" and "lords" didn't try to actively raise it.

That's where the key to the Taoist tenet of *wu wei* really lies. Obviously, you should plan ahead and strategize your crowd-funding campaign, and that takes effort. Obviously you should put a fair amount of thought into your invitation video, story, incentives, and promotional tactics. And obviously this is what this entire book has been telling you all along. But if you go with the flow of your film and follow through in your campaign strategy, you avoid overexerting yourself, and *that* is the real message behind this frequently misinterpreted Taoist principle.

The same is true for when you start promoting your crowd-funding campaign on Facebook, Twitter, Instagram, and various other social media sites. You should exercise *wei wu wei*, or "doing without doing." This may seem like a paradox at first glance, but not if you examine it in a slightly larger sense before we dive into its relationship to the microcosm of crowdfunding. Think of it as going with the flow of the social media universe, much like how planets rotate and revolve around the sun. They don't question it. Venus doesn't try to compete with Mars or Earth for the shortest amount of rotations around the sun. The planets simply do what they need to do, and as a result the whole galaxy is kept in balance. It's only when you try to upset that balance that things become difficult and ultimately fall apart.

Back to crowdfunding: You can view the concept of *wei wu wei* as simply knowing when to interact and when to promote your campaign. Sometimes we can overdo the promotion and flood our friends' feeds, but oftentimes we allow our own thoughts to dictate whether we'll overdo it *before* ever even doing it. Confused? You're thinking too hard, and thought is the enemy of action and non-action. Don't worry — we'll clear up this confusion in these next few chapters, which will show you how to navigate the vast social mediascape without disturbing the universe too much as you inch closer to your goal.

• • •

Chapter Twenty-Eight

TWITTER TIPS FOR CROWDFUNDING FILMMAKERS

IF YOU WERE trying to spread word about your film in the days before the Internet, you would probably have needed to spend lots of money on print material like flyers, postcards, and business cards to hand out to people. More money spent on those elements meant less money when you completed your fundraising, more physical waste, and more time spent doing something other than making your film. But we're fortunate to live in a time that's made interactions and promotion as easy as sending an email or updating one's Facebook status. There's no longer a need to include with your business card a mini CD-ROM or even a flash drive showing off your trailer. A potential contributor can now simply watch it right from his or her phone.

Twitter, in particular, has become one of the most powerful tools for spreading the word about your crowdfunding campaign since it forces you to be concise and to think in what's referred to as "tweetable quotes," which someone else might easily remember, repeat, and ultimately retweet. It's also powerful because of its real-time nature; the second you get news, you can share it right at that moment and it can reach thousands of people within the next minute, if you know how to maximize your outreach into the vast Twitterverse.

That said, Twitter is not a social media platform that comes naturally to most filmmakers, so here are a few key tips I've taken away from my own experiences crowdfunding *Cerise* and consulting on many other campaigns that did it right.

BE A PROLOGUE BEFORE YOU PETITION

I joined Twitter on May 4, 2009. I began crowdfunding for *Cerise* on February 2, 2010, nine months after I had birthed a modest following of about 200 or so Twitter users. The first people I started following were friends, of course. Then I started searching hashtags (#film and #filmmaking at first) and following Twitter users like @gregorybayne and @kingisafink — people who shared interests similar to mine. It wasn't long before I was engaging in meaningful 140-character conversations about obscure directors like Alejandro Jodorowsky and sharing my insights on filmmaking, screenwriting, and storytelling with people who followed my tweets.

It would later be these same followers who would make up my core of initial backers for *Cerise*. Had I not given myself ample time to genuinely get to know these individuals, to forge actual relationships instead of just networks, I doubt that many of them would have felt a desire to contribute $50 or more to my campaign. People give to people, yes, but do people give to strangers? Yes — you may give a quarter, even a dollar, to the less fortunate, but not $25 or $50. Therefore, you should avoid being misconstrued as someone who has set up a Twitter account for the sole purpose of promoting his or her crowdfunding campaign. Nothing spells *spamateur* more than that.

CREATIVITY IS KING

Because you've only got 140 characters with which to capture your potential contributors' attention (this may change as Twitter evolves), it's important to be as creative as possible when composing your tweets. It takes a little more time, but your followers will appreciate it. They'll see that you're not a @CampaignerBot flooding them with the same tweet over and over again about your film's campaign, but an actual person who painstakingly crafts each and every tweet as an affirmation of the passion you feel for it.

Sometimes even the most creative tweeters and retweeters come out with more run-of-the-mill tweets, like Leilani Holmes' tweet for *Clowning Around*, which is actually the generic tweet that Indiegogo sets up for you: "Help make it happen for *Clowning Around* on #Indiegogo." This isn't a very compelling tweet, truth be told, and even Indiegogo knows this, which is why once you click "Tweet" from its sharing toolbar, everything gets highlighted except the link for easy deleting so you can write your own, more personal message. There's no excuse for anyone not to have a little fun with his or her promotion, like crowdfunding champ Gavin ap'Morrygan (@Tearsinrain78) and supporter Graham Inman (@grahaminman) did here for the same project:

 Tearsinrain78 Gavin apmorrygan
Get your tix to the circus RT @grahaminman: Bonzo and a Bottle on Clowning Around on #indiegogo igg.me/p/6492?a=53624…
#clowningaroundfilm
3 Aug

28.1. *A playful tweet by @TearsinRain78 and @grahaminman during the campaign for the short film* Clowning Around.

KEEP OUT OF "THE LOOP"

Even a quirky tweet like Gavin and Graham's can lose its charm and freshness if your followers see the same exact tweet three times in a row from three different people. If you have a personal Twitter account and a separate handle for your film, do your followers a favor and keep them separate. Linking your personal and film or production company accounts can be detrimental to your crowdfunding efforts. People don't like to hear the same things twice, and chances are the majority of your followers are also following your film's Twitter. If your accounts are linked, your tweets will soon become redundant. It becomes even more perilous to a crowdfunding campaign if you have several members of your team on Twitter *and* your film all linked together. Then it becomes spam. Therefore, you should strive to put in the extra effort and make every tweet from every account something special and worth reading.

ALWAYS INCLUDE YOUR (SHORTENED) LINK

Whenever you tweet about your film campaign, you should always include a link to it so that the first thing a potential contributor sees after he or she clicks the link is your invitation video. Because links can be pretty lengthy at times, and on Twitter, every letter and space is precious, you should always use a link–shortening service like Bit.ly, Ow.ly and Google's own link shortener, or even the native shortening that most crowdfunding platforms offer, which will allow you the freedom to be creative in your tweets and supply your followers with a link to your campaign.

#HASHTAG #EVERYTHING #RELEVANT TO YOUR #PROJECT

In every tweet you send, be sure to hashtag words and phrases related to your project and campaign. This makes it easy for random people far from your own following to find your campaign on Twitter or even through a Google search. Here's a great example from Meg Pinsonneault's documentary *Gwapa (Beautiful)*:

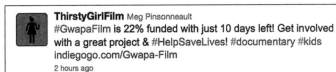

ThirstyGirlFilm Meg Pinsonneault
#GwapaFilm is 22% funded with just 10 days left! Get involved with a great project & #HelpSaveLives! #documentary #kids
indiegogo.com/Gwapa-Film
2 hours ago

28.2. Meg Pinsonnealt's tweet for Gwapa (Beautiful) *makes excellent use of hashtags to reach various audiences.*

Right away, I know that this is a #documentary about #kids, and there's an urgency to #HelpSaveLives. Meg and her team also switched up their hashtags each time they tweeted about

#GwapaFilm; some tweets will highlight #Filipino, since this is a documentary about helping the children of two Filipino families who have cleft lip or cleft palate. Other tweets focused on the film's #inspirational nature.

The first thing you'll want to do is to find out what words or phrases relevant to your film bring specific communities together on Twitter. Think of these as little galaxies in a vast cosmos of galaxies. The easiest way to find a specific community is to plug in the coordinates (hashtags) into your "navicomputer" and you'll reach your destination. For making movies, I've found that #film, #indiefilm, #supportindiefilm, and #filmmaking are all popular hashtags for connecting to these communities. If you're raising money for a short film about an underdog who becomes a king in a fantasy world, I would hashtag all of the above, plus #fantasy and #underdog for direct access to those groups, as well as #sci-fi and #shortfilm to indirectly make your way into related communities.

You don't want to hashtag more than about two or three things per tweet, though, so save different words for different tweets. According to @TheCounter (posted in June 2015), tweets that have one or two hashtags have a 21% increase in engagement, whereas tweets using three or more hashtags show a 17% decrease in engagement. So space out your use of hashtags the way you would space out your tweets for maximum interactions between the people you want to reach.

REMEMBER — DON'T SOLICIT, ELICIT

I introduced this "Golden Rule" back in Chapter Twenty, and I've included it as a Twitter tip as well because this is doubly true when using this particular social network. Simply asking people to visit your Indiegogo or Kickstarter page will only get you so far in your campaign, and it may even get you all the way to your crowdfunding goal. But if your aim is to raise upward of $25,000, you'll most likely need to expand your network. The way to do that is to start eliciting responses from potential contributors if you want to bring in larger contributions and a handful of retweets from your network that are more personal than a click of the "Retweet" button.

Here's an example of a tweet that solicits, or asks, for help, from filmmaker Will Warner for his web series: "Please help me to fund my next film *Tales of the Black Ghost*." Again, there's nothing wrong with a tweet like this, of course, but it's too similar to the typical "Make it happen for (fill in your campaign here)" Indiegogo tweet. Now look at this tweet from Wonder Russell that elicits or evokes a response: "A small town pizza girl. Gary Busey. Seattle Indie. Let's Finish *Jenny*."

Obviously, this tweet for finishing funds for Sam Graydon's *Jenny* is meant to intrigue and make you want to click the link to see what this campaign is all about. So as much as possible throughout your crowdfunding campaign, elicit responses from your followers because you'll more than likely elicit something more tangible than a $10 or $100 contribution.

@EVERYBODY

Whenever you thank a contributor, be sure to mention (@) that person on Twitter. If you're not sure if he or she has a Twitter account or don't know that person's handle, do a quick Google search of that person's name and "on Twitter" and you'll probably find him or her fairly easy. Even if the person you're thanking doesn't sign in to Twitter very often or even if his or her little pastel egg of a profile picture hasn't hatched into the person you know and follow, you should show your appreciation as a campaigner nonetheless so it's on the record, transparent and in plain sight of everyone.

Make Things Easier with a Twitter Client

If Twitter is going to be a hub where a hefty amount of your promotion will stem from, then I recommend making your life easier by working with a Twitter client, which is basically an app that makes tweeting (and even Facebook updating and other social media output) a cinch. Two of the more widely used ones are Hootsuite and Tweetdeck, and there are also a number of pay services like Sprout Social, which are good if you're planning to manage more than one Twitter account.

Perhaps the most convenient aspect of any Twitter client is the ability to schedule tweets, which can make crowdfunding a bit less stressful. If you know you have a full day of work ahead of you at the day job, you can schedule some tweets about your film's campaign the night before. This way, through the course of the day, you will still appear to be tweeting and promoting your campaign. But beware: Scheduled tweets should follow the same rules previously mentioned; otherwise, you may stumble into the realm of the @SpamBot, and your followers may start to ignore your campaigning by muting you in their Twitter stream or unfollowing you completely. This is why it's important to schedule tweets that vary from one to the other.

One thing you cannot schedule, however, are interactions — you've got to be ever present for those, because you never know which ones might manifest into a stronger relationship and a contribution to your film campaign. The minute you receive a tweet from someone and it warrants a response, respond right away.

That said, your presence on Twitter as a crowdfunder is really all about personalization. You should be sure to maintain a steady presence on Twitter while you're campaigning by interacting with your followers in ways unrelated to your #filmcampaign. Again, people give to people, not bots. Once you nurture and maintain those relationships as a person and a crowdfunder, you will build a network that will walk beside a person they'll be proud to know and support in the future.

Chapter Twenty-Nine

• • •

FACEBOOK PAGES, EVENTS, AND "FRIEND FAWNING"

FACEBOOK, LIKE TWITTER, has proven an invaluable tool for film-makers crowdfunding their movies. Like Twitter, you can update your status to reflect what you're doing at the moment you're doing it. You can also post photos and videos, you can like other people's statuses, share content you find interesting with your friends, or post directly to a friend's wall. You can create photo albums so you will always remember your most important life events. You can even poke people to remind them that you're there.

Because Facebook is one of the few social media platforms that constantly innovates on a regular basis, you'll want to keep up to date with any new features that Facebook unveils and see if you can use them for your crowdfunding. Aside from simply updating statuses and posting content relevant to your film campaign, there are a few other helpful things you may want to consider. You can set up a Facebook page and/or event for your film, send messages, and even engage in this somewhat controversial tactic I've affec-tionately termed "friend fawning."

FACEBOOK PAGES

Setting up a Facebook page for your film is simple enough, but before you jump into filling in all the pertinent details about it, you may want to make certain of three key things: First, that you have time to update your film's Facebook page; second, that you have enough content with which to update the page; and third, that you're willing to invest some money in Facebook ads and/

or boosted posts. I mention these because there's a difference between engagement, maintenance, and stagnation. The latter won't help you with your crowdfunding campaign in any way if your Facebook page is just lifelessly collecting e-dust. Maintenance usually means updating a status once a day or posting a photo every week or two, but this will give people little reason to like your page. Engagement, on the other hand, will show that things are moving forward at a proper pace, which will also boost your social proof, having friends and those who like your film's page actively participate in its success.

Once you've finished the initial steps of setting up your Facebook page and have added a profile pic, cover photo, and some basic information like a synopsis, website URL, and a list of the people responsible for your film, it's time to build awareness of your page. The easiest way to do this is to invite each and every one of your Facebook friends to like your film page, and you should do this long before your campaign launches. The whole purpose of having a Facebook page is to build further awareness of the film, not your crowdfunding campaign.

Another way to get word out quickly about your film's Facebook page is to link your Facebook page's updates to Twitter. Now you might be thinking to yourself *but didn't you just tell me in the previous chapter* not *to connect your Twitter and Facebook accounts?!* Yes, I did. But with your Facebook page, it's a bit different. If you connect your personal Facebook profile with your movie's Twitter account, for instance, every single update you post will be a tweet, whether or not it's related to your film and/or campaign. If you're posting as *Sync* the Movie on Facebook, however, and the corresponding tweet is being sent out from @SyncMovie, that's marketing. But if your Facebook page and Twitter account are also linked to your personal page or Twitter account, then it becomes spam of the first magnitude and should be avoided.

One of the only snags with linking your film's Facebook and Twitter accounts is that you'll ultimately blur the invisible line between these two diverse social networks. For instance, even though Facebook uses them, hashtags are more widely used on Twitter and Instagram, but you'll have to include them in your status updates if you want those hashtags to appear on Twitter, where they are most useful. You can also post additional tweets directly from Twitter that include hashtags and mentions, but if you're in a pinch for time, doing it from Facebook will save some valuable minutes. My suggestion, however, is to tweet a tweet, update a Facebook status, and keep them separate, if time permits, of course.

One thing to be aware of is that running a Facebook page properly will cost you some money. Facebook is a business, and sees your film as such, so they charge you money to be able to reach more of your fans and even to spread the word beyond your fans and friends. That's where boosted posts, in which you pay per post to reach more of your fan base, and Facebook-promoted posts, which are more like standard ads appearing in your timeline, come into play, though for a campaign raising $10,000 to $30,000, you probably don't have to worry about that just yet. We'll chat in Chapter Thirty-Four about raising $100,000 to $1M in crowdfunding. That's when Facebook ad spends are a must.

Okay, so how does having a Facebook page up and active during your film's crowdfunding campaign benefit your efforts? Most importantly, it will build up your audience and draw in new potential contributors to your campaign. If they visit the page and like it, then discover from a status update that you're crowdfunding, they may click the link to your campaign, which for the time being should be listed as your film's website as well, and contribute a few dollars to a film that they like and would probably enjoy watching in the future.

Cerise is an interesting exception with regard to its Facebook page. My team and I didn't have one until *after* the film was shot and in the editing room, mainly because crowdfunding was time-consuming enough for us without having to worry about updating our own Facebook accounts *and* the movie's page. If you feel that it may be too much, you can opt to start your film's page after crowdfunding is complete. If you have someone who can take care of those updates for you, then an active Facebook page while crowdfunding can only enhance your outreach and attract even more potential contributors to your crowdfunding campaign.

But remember to always keep your personal touch touching others. This is your film we're talking about marketing, not a real estate agency.

FACEBOOK EVENTS

Many crowdfunders also set up a Facebook event to further build awareness for their campaign. This is a great way to gauge a person's interest in participating in your online fundraising; you'll get an idea of who's "Going," who "Can't Go," and who's "Interested," though the semantics may change with time. ("Interested" used to be "Maybe" not too long ago.)

But Facebook events can also be useful as an alternative to having to pay for boosted and promoted posts on Facebook and allows you to reach more of the audience you've earned for your film. With an event, you have most of the same functionality that you do on a page, like the ability to post updates, photos, and videos to all your invitees, but they come without the costs now associated with pages.

Setting up a Facebook event for your indie film's crowdfunding campaign isn't as simple as plugging in some info and inviting your friends. As with anything related to marketing and crowdfunding, you need to make sure your event stands out from the others out there, so here are a few things to consider when setting one up:

- **Name**: Come up with a snazzy title that will make people not want to miss out, as if this was an actual physical event. "Support *Apocalypse Rock* until the End of Days!" would be a smart, eye-catching title. The name of your film simply won't do.

- **Details**: Keep it short and sweet on your event page, and word it in such a way that your invitees will want to visit your crowdfunding campaign for the full details about your film, and will also be able to fund it while they're there.

- **Where**: This one is *very* important. This is where your crowdfunding campaign's short link should go, to make it very easy for everyone to click and go to it so they can go fund it.

- **When**: This one's simple — set this as the duration dates of your campaign.

- **Privacy**: You can make your event "Public" or set it to "Open Invite." In that case, anyone you invite can also invite others, and this can be an extremely valuable feature if you can get those initial invitees spreading the word about your campaign to their friends.

Now, just as important as setting up your event properly is making sure to keep the event alive and thriving with updates about your film campaign, which will go out to all those who are going to the event. Perhaps the only difficulty here is that there probably won't be any giveaways, dancing, and free booze. But what you *can* offer is a deeper connection to the campaign and the film, the same way we used to do with a Facebook page, and with Facebook constantly mucking things up for filmmakers and crowdfunders alike, we need to constantly be on the lookout for new ways of engaging our friends and fan base by having a place to congregate in a virtual setting.

And what better way than inviting them to the main "event" to stay up and party with us and make a movie?

FRIEND FAWNING

This brings us to the final approach on how to really bring in the contributions to your crowdfunding campaign from Facebook, but be warned: This one is *not* for the faint of heart. In fact, out of *Cerise*'s modest team of three, I was the only one who felt comfortable enough doing this without worrying about how many friends I might lose in the process. No one, no matter how devout they are about filmmaking, will be as passionate and no-holds-barred about your film campaign as you are.

This tactic was spawned during *Cerise*'s second lull. To quell this quietude, I started sending personal Facebook messages one by one to friends I had been interacting with for a while, and this tactic worked to bring in some more contributions. But there were so many people I had messaged who weren't getting back to me. Then I had one now ex-acquaintance who kindly asked me to stop messaging her, and I suddenly got worried that my crowdfunding efforts so far were all for naught. But as with everything else regarding filmmaking and life, it's not about quitting, it's about figuring out new ways to approach a problem and deal with it. I didn't know how this particular solution would affect my Facebook friendships, but I decided to risk it because I believed *that* strongly in my film.

That said, I introduce to you a Facebook tactic I've named "friend fawning," which is basically writing directly on your individual friends' walls about your film campaign. At first, this may seem invasive — it's one thing to post a YouTube video that you found enjoyable and thought your friend might also find it so; it's quite another to post a link to your Indiegogo or Kickstarter campaign on his or her wall for not only that person, but for all of his or her friends to see as well. But as I learned, it's all about *how* you present yourself and your campaign in that post.

First things first, though: You shouldn't ever write on a brand-new friend's timeline seeking funding for your film — only friends and acquaintances you've had for a while and with whom you interact at least every now and again, because the key to what makes friend fawning work is forming a connection in a single wall post. This is a threefold process, much like recording your invitation video: There's the *greeting*, followed by the *personal touch*, and finally, the *invitation*.

For *Cerise*, I started out with a standard greeting like, "Hey Jim, it's been a while, huh?" I like to start with a question because I find most people will respond to an inquiry rather than a statement like "It's been way too long!" Then, I'd search for something on their page that I could mention to show that I've been keeping up with their lives, even though at the time it may not have been entirely true. Usually, this was something related to one of their latest status updates, and it would be something like, "I can't believe your son's walking already — That's awesome!" That's the personal touch.

Then comes the invitation. This requires a smooth transition from the personal touch — which is all about your friend — to the invite, which is all about you and your film campaign. Perhaps transition with something along the lines of, "I know you've got your hands full with your family, but... " and then dive into a concise invite: "... I'm raising funds for my next film and I'd really appreciate if you could help out with $5. Check out my page." Then, of course, include the link to your crowdfunding campaign.

Occasionally, I'd put a very low dollar amount like $5, and most people would contribute at least $10 since that was the starting contribution. Sometimes I wouldn't put any dollar amount, and instead I would simply tell them "there are a lot of cool perks for different dollar amounts." Other times, I would highlight the most personal perk for *Cerise*, which was the acrostic poem, and leave it at that. These frequent change-ups of the wording will keep your wall posts from registering on your friends' radars as spam, as well as show that there's an actual person behind each post.

There will be some friends who will not answer these wall posts at all. There'll even be some who delete it. But many will respond because people value the friendships they have on Facebook, especially if you're friends outside of Facebook. Others may answer because they might be wondering things like *how long has this post been on my wall?* and *how many of* my *friends have seen this post already?* They won't want to look bad to their friends if they refuse to reply in some way to your post.

How often should you fawn your friends on Facebook? I follow the rule of three in just about everything, and this is no different. If I posted about *Cerise* one week, I waited about five days before I posted another message and link on the same person's wall. If that person didn't reply to it by then, I waited a full week and posted once more. After a third time and still no reply, I figured he or she didn't want to be bothered by me or my film, or he or she had unfriended or even blocked me by then, which is essentially the same. At least with *Cerise*, I very rarely had to fawn the same friend more than once, and I was very happy with the contributions that amounted due to this tactic. Some friends gave $10, but many gave a minimum of $50, which really helped get me to my goal much faster.

It seems like a lot of work at first glance, but in all honesty, it's not, if you've got your eye on the prize — the goal for your film campaign. In terms of *wei wu wei*, this is really doing without doing. If we're a part of a social network like Facebook, and we're viewing our friends' status updates, that means we want to know what these friends are up to. In this sense, we're simply going with the flow and interacting with our friends — the primary difference being when we're crowdfunding, we have a stronger reason to interact. As controversial as it may seem to some, it's because of friend fawning that I've taken a more genuine interest in everything that my friends are posting on Facebook, and I now make sure to take a few minutes out of every day to keep updated on projects, family milestones, and recent photos and videos.

We are all part of a community, after all.

Chapter Thirty

...

INSTAGRAM FOR CROWDFUNDING FILMMAKERS

As FILMMAKERS, WE know that it's pretty mandatory to be active on Facebook and Twitter. And even though there are dozens of other platforms, we should pick and choose a few of the ones we can make the most out of with regard to promoting our films and ourselves. Depending on the audience for your film, you may decide to pin to your heart's content on Pinterest, cater to the modern-age attention span with Snapchats, or even get hyper local with Yik Yak and record and reply to waves on Anchor.

And then there's Instagram.

While all those others are your choice, as a filmmaker, you should certainly be making the most of your Instagram account as much as you do your Facebook and Twitter. This is especially true with regard to crowdfunding an indie film, yet most filmmakers don't realize its importance and its ease just yet, since Instagram natively speaks a photographic language that should cater to all visual content creators.

That said, here's a mini how-to guide to get you started using your Instagram for crowdfunding your film.

INSTAGRAM YOUR INCENTIVES

This is probably the easiest way to try to drive actual funds into your crowdfunding campaign. The whole point of Instagram is to post images for people to like, and if you've got some cool incentives to offer, snap some eye-catching pictures and post them.

ADD WORDS AND DESIGN TO YOUR PHOTOS

A picture alone won't speak enough words to make someone actually *buy* that perk or reward. Use apps like InstaSize and Studio, which is a bit more advanced, to add a bit more design to those images, create memes, and entice your followers to not only like the image, but also to contribute to your campaign and nab that incentive. You can also use Instagram's Layout and Boomerang apps to create more engaging layouts and GIFs.

30.1. *A little design goes a long way: Here's an image I use on Twitter whenever I share this Medium post.*

SHOOT VIDEO UPDATES

Are you doing a Reddit AMA? Did you just land an actor whom everyone knows? Instagram's fifteen-second video feature is awesome for shooting very quick updates or even teasers for these kinds of events and announcements. It's also an opportunity for you to get out from behind the camera once again and get personal with your followers and contributors.

PUT TOGETHER A FIFTEEN-SECOND #INSTATRAILER

If you're crowdfunding for postproduction funds, and if you've got some footage of the film, even if it's not color corrected and sound designed (which it shouldn't be, since that's what you're crowdfunding for), you can cut quite a compelling fifteen-second trailer for the film. Cut a few of them, since content is king and campaigning can be long. For great examples of Instatrailers, check out what @FilmShortage has been doing with the films they feature, like Kevan Funk's *Destroyer* (a personal favorite of mine).

INSTAMINISERIES

I *wish* I could take credit for this awesome amalgam, but it's really from a pair of hip young women who are doing some really cool and innovative stuff with their Instagram account. They're paying homage to the silent films of Chaplin and Keaton with a fresh twist in *Silent Brokelyn*. Now, they're not crowdfunding per se, but if they were, I'm sure they'd still be producing free content for folks to view while they raise funds for a future Instaminiseries.

KNOW THE RIGHT HASHTAGS

One cool thing about Instagram — well, there are a lot of cool things about Instagram — is that the more tags you use (Instagram allows you up to thirty hashtags), the wider reach you have, versus Twitter, where adding more than two tags can statistically *limit* your organic reach. The only caveat? You need to know the *right* tags to use. Foodies, for instance, love using a ton of tags, but there's a difference between "#eeeeeats" and "#eeeeeeeats," and now no one even uses the right one anymore. Be sure to use the right one the first time so it always pops up as a suggestion in your subsequent film posts.

Documentary filmmakers have the added advantage of not only tapping into the #indiefilm community on Instagram, but also an audience interested in the subject of the documentary. Be doubly sure to discover all the right tags early on so you can establish yourself as a subject matter expert and establish your Instagram account as a resource for learning more about that subject.

DIRECT PEOPLE TO THE LINK IN YOUR BIO

One of the things I actually really love about Instagram (though this may change over time) is that it doesn't allow links except in your bio. That means if you want people to check out your actual crowdfunding campaign, you have to direct them to the "link in my bio" with each and every post. (Unless you choose to go the paid ad route, which does allow click-throughs right from the image.) And they will take that extra step, *if* your photo is worth the click.

And during a crowdfunding campaign, that means putting the campaign's short link as your website, because when you're crowdfunding an indie film, that's the site that matters most for the duration of the campaign.

IT'S CALLED INSTAGRAM, NOT *SPAM*-STAGRAM

Be professional with your promotion and remember that Instagram is about sharing images and videos that matter, and unlike Twitter or Facebook, posting once is enough, as long as what you post showcases the best of what you've got.

Now that you've got this brief guide to Instagram at your fingertips, go out there and start snapping shots, hashtagging #cinematography and other tags, and building up your following so you've got a captive audience once you start crowdfunding your indie film.

Chapter Thirty-One

• • •

MOBILE CROWDFUNDING, BROADCASTING, AND EMERGING FORMS OF SOCIAL MEDIA

The fact is that the social media landscape changes very quickly from year to year. Today's hot platform could be ousted tomorrow as mayor of the public's attention, and unless you're reading TechCrunch on a regular basis, it's difficult to know what the next hit social media site will be. Not to mention the fact that the forms these social networks take change rapidly. Yesterday's image-based Instagram could be replaced by tomorrow's Vine.

That's why it's very good practice to stay up to date with not only what's popular, but what's probably going to be popular in the months to come. While it's impossible to know for sure which ones will be successful and which ones will have promise but for one reason or another not catch on (Google Plus, anyone?), here are a few things to consider for crowdfunding today and tomorrow.

EVERYTHING'S GOING MOBILE

As human beings adapt, so does social media. Like many things on the Internet, what began as an at-home-only activity with people seated at their desktop computers led them to trade in their towers for laptops; slowly laptops are going the way of the dodo in favor of smartphones and tablets. And just as more and more people every year are checking their Facebook statuses, retweeting articles, and posting and pinning photos to Instagram and Pinterest in real time or as a #latergram right from their phones, more people are making purchases on e-commerce sites (Amazon), sending money to friends (Venmo), and doing just about everything "on the go."

Therefore, it's important to be versatile and adapt your crowdfunding to the shifting landscape that's quickly going from desktop to mobile applications. The big crowdfunding platforms like Indiegogo, Kickstarter, and GoFundMe already have apps for iOS and Android, and they have optimized their sites for a great mobile experience as well, making crowdfunding on the go for your indie film much easier. In fact, you could be on-set setting up a shot and get a notification that someone has just contributed to your campaign and thank that person within seconds. You can type out and send an update unveiling a new incentive or just to say thanks to all the backers who have already contributed to making your next film the best one yet.

BROADCASTING: PERISCOPE AND MEERKAT

What began with Skype and Google Hangouts on Air has in recent years evolved into live broadcasting through mobile apps like Periscope and Meerkat. This has become a popular trend and proves a fundamental principle not only about crowdfunding an indie film, but also about social media and its evolution: People. Want. *Access*. And today, we can give them that access on a scale never before seen.

Take the Indiegogo for *Con Man*, a web series from the main actors behind *Firefly*, Alan Tudyk and Nathan Fillion. (Full disclosure here: I was the campaign strategist working behind the scenes with the producer PJ Haarsma and the campaign manager helping to make it a successful multimillion-dollar campaign.) As part of their outreach and one of their low-tier perks, they gave their fans access to them via the broadcasting app Hang With, which is a little less well known than Meerkat and Periscope, but basically the same. Every now and again, Alan, Nathan, and PJ or *Con Man* itself would go live to make some announcements pertaining to the Indiegogo or the series, or just to hang out and shout out some folks who had tuned into the broadcast.

Broadcasting builds a stronger social bridge between you, your audience, and your film. Again, social media is becoming more and more about granting access; about pulling back the metaphorical curtain so that your backers get to see what goes on *behind* that curtain, to see all the wizards of Oz at work on the films they've supported with their dollars.

GET READY — VIRTUAL REALITY IS COMING

There's a great line in the 1989 *Batman* movie, in which Jack Napier tells Lieutenant Eckhardt that he "ought to think about the future." And of course, by "think about" we really mean keep it in mind and always know that just when we get used to one way of doing something, right around the corner lies something brand-new that will change it all, usually for the better. Crowdfunding an indie film is no different.

The more multimedia evolves, the more immersive it will become, and the more technologies will emerge that seek to capture this immersion and deliver it to an audience that wants it. I won't spend much more time delving into the various technologies that make virtual reality possible today, but I do want to get across that a good general must have a clear knowledge of what's coming and how to use it to his advantage before it becomes his disadvantage. This can be mostly seen in things like virtual reality. From a crowdfunding perspective, a future in which our audiences will be experiencing just about everything through a pair of VR goggles like the Oculus isn't that far off, and it's not just for gamers and *The Lawnmower Man* anymore.

With every year that passes, the things we once deemed as science fiction drop the "fiction" part and become science *fact*. The day when a crowdfunding perk for a film about surrogates could be to upload the contributor's consciousness into the film's robot protagonist isn't as far-fetched as you may think. Okay, maybe *that's* a little out there, but a reward that allows a backer to experience what it's like to have a landmine explode a few feet away from you in an augmented 1943 Germany for your World War II period piece, or to feel the weightlessness of space in your indie sci-fi epic are just around the corner and will be here before we know it.

The question you as a crowdfunding filmmaker will need to ask is what kind of incentives can you offer to immerse potential contributors into the storyworld of your indie film? For this, even the greatest 3-D! incentive wouldn't be enough. No, we would need to implement a *fourth* type of crowdfunding incentive — the *Virtual/Real (V/R)* — which would give your backers so much access that they would literally be brought into the world of your indie film. But we'll talk more about that in the third edition.

SOCIAL MEDIA TO KEEP AN EYE ON

Okay, back to the present reality. There are some well-established social media sites that have not proven to be a very strong asset for crowdfunding campaigns. Yet.

LinkedIn

When the first edition of *Crowdfunding for Filmmakers* was released, I did a bunch of signings and seminars throughout New York and New Jersey. At one such event, an older gentleman asked a question about LinkedIn and how people are using this more professional social network for crowdfunding. I replied simply with "they're not," to which he returned with "but that's where the *big money* is."

That was years ago, and to this day, I still don't see LinkedIn bringing any "big money" to crowdfunded films or anything else.

But it doesn't mean it can't one day. And while I would say that this person's mind was focused on the wrong part of the compound word that is "crowdfunding," with LinkedIn becoming its own mechanism for getting messages out to a wider audience through native blogs, for instance, it's a good idea to keep an eye on it, since it could become a viable outlet for crowdfunding a film.

Reddit

What this veritable treasure trove of information lacks in user friendliness it makes up for by being a major platform for spreading word about your indie film's crowdfunding campaign farther out toward its target audience. The Ask Me Anything (AMA) is perhaps Reddit's most popular feature, and many campaigns, from *Black Angel* to *Super Troopers 2* have done them. The thing is, Reddit is a community in the purest sense of the word, and this community does not abide straight sales. That is, when you do an AMA, you cannot blatantly promote your Indiegogo or Kickstarter campaign. You must talk about your film, the making of it, the process of writing it — anything that is not a solicitation or even an elicitation for contributions.

Snapchat

If you're looking to make an indie film whose audience is thirty-four years old or younger,, then you *need* to be on Snapchat and figure out how best to engage this particular demographic with your content. Well-known brands like Food Network, Vice, and CNN have been making huge strides in figuring out how best to engage with an audience within five and ten seconds, and so should we as crowdfunding filmmakers.

SOCIAL MEDIA OF CROWDFUNDING'S FUTURE

There will always be a new social media platform, or one that suddenly rises in popularity after being dormant for a time. Some of them will cater to specific demographics. Others will make it easier to reach out to the people who will help carve out your *Pu* and make your campaign a success. The key is to always remember that what we currently have at our fingertips as tools is not the be-all and end-all, but the beginning of something more to come. The wise crowdfunder knows to always be in the present tense, yet to keep a keen eye on what's to come so he or she can quickly figure out how to make the most out of it when crowdfunding.

Chapter Thirty-Two

• • •

A Few Should-Nots of Social Media for Crowdfunding

Taoism is about finding the positive in everything and nurturing it to benefit you and the world around you. The same holds true with crowdfunding. So far I've been focusing on the positive things that filmmakers should do to successfully crowdfund their films, but balance dictates that where there's a positive, there's also a negative, or else the former couldn't exist. When promoting our campaigns heavily on social media, we constantly run the risk of going overboard and falling off the tightrope into the dark side of promotion: spam.

The following are a few do-nots of social media for crowdfunding, or rather a few *should-nots*, since doing them won't automatically excommunicate you from your indie film and crowdfunding circles. These are some things you should avoid simply to keep the experience of crowdfunding positive for you, your potential contributors, and your most ardent supporters.

Friend Fouling

Continuing with Facebook, as mentioned in Chapter Twenty-Nine, my friend fawning tactic, in which you post your link directly onto your friends' walls, is questionable at best, but there's a difference between friend fawning and "friend fouling," the Mr. Hyde to the former's Dr. Jekyll. The difference is simple: Posting *only* a link to your crowdfunding campaign on your friend's page can be construed as rude, especially if you haven't spoken to this friend in quite a while or if you've only recently become friends on Facebook. You don't want to purposely foul up your friendships, especially before you nurture them into a trusted network.

EXECUTIVE PRODUCER: A(NOTHER) CROWDFUNDER HAS SENT YOU A FRIEND REQUEST

This one's a biggie. So big I'm using the words "do not" to show how big a point this is. If you see that someone has contributed a substantial amount of money to a single campaign and thus has become an executive producer, *do not* send that person a friend request right away. Once that contributor checks you out, he or she'll quickly discover that you are also currently crowdfunding for a film and may jump to the (correct) assumption that you're adding him or her in the hopes that he or she might contribute a similar amount to your campaign.

This actually did happen. A friend of mine who was crowdfunding his indie romantic comedy noticed that a few people had contributed to *Cerise*, so he sent them a friend request on Facebook right away. Since I make a point to talk with my backers on a regular basis, a couple of them asked me if I knew this person. Once I asked why, they mentioned that he added them as a friend, but they saw that he was crowdfunding as well and unfriended him. They felt that it was a bit shady of that person to try to jump on the funding bandwagon while the money they gave to *Cerise* was still hot from their pockets. And they were absolutely right. That's bad practice in any arena.

IT'S CALLED PROMOTION, NOT SPAM-MOTION

Much the same way you shouldn't set up your crowdfunding campaign and let it languish until potential contributors happen upon your film project, you shouldn't assail your friends and supporters with unrelenting activity. You should always strive to be a pro when planning out your promotional tactics to avoid the pitfalls of those annoying "Need Cash Now?" advertisements that are texted to people's phones. In the past, when a telemarketer foisted their unfortunate phone calls upon us, we would simply hang up until they got the message. Since the dawn of Facebook and Twitter, such an annoyance is swiftly resolved by clicking the "Unfriend" or "Unfollow" buttons, and in that moment, you lose not only a friend or follower, but also a possible supporter. When you disturb the universe, it seeks to balance itself once more, and it will be balanced at the expense of your film project. There's a fine line between promotion and spam-motion. There's an even finer line between marketing and desperation.

Since you must promote your film campaign, you should always strive to remain personable in your publicity, and by doing so you steer clear of those dastardly "Report Spam" and "Block" features that get plenty of use on our social networks. Do this, and you'll see firsthand that the personal touch most often leads to the Midas touch.

• Part Five •
Summary Points

- *Wei wu wei* is the Taoist principle of non-action, literally "doing without doing." In a crowdfunding sense, this can be translated to doing without *over*doing.

- With promotion on Twitter, there are a few important things to remember, such as always including a shortened link to your campaign's homepage, hashtagging everything relevant to your film, and, of course, eliciting rather than soliciting.

- Facebook has plenty of helpful tools crowdfunders can use to get the word out about their films, including pages and events.

- "Friend fawning" (writing on friends' Facebook walls) is a controversial tactic, but it can be made less controversial by including a greeting, personal touch, and then an invitation in every message you post directly onto a friend's wall.

- Instagram comes with its own set of best practices for crowd-funding, like snapping shots of your incentives, creating fifteen-second Instatrailers, and unveiling new contests and updates visually. #NoFilter Needed.

- Always keep a keen eye on the present *and* future and find ways to use other forms of social media like Snapchat, Meerkat, or the Oculus Rift (and whatever might arise after that, too).

- Amongst some of the crowdfunding should-nots are "friend fouling" (posting only the link to your campaign on someone's Facebook wall) and adding executive producers because they gave a substantial amount to another project.

• PART FIVE •
EXERCISES

1. "Friend fawning" vs. "friend fouling" — Write up three mock wall posts. Be sure to include the following:

    a) a warm greeting;

    b) a personal touch, something specific about the friend that shows you've been keeping up with his or her Facebook feed;

    c) a smooth transition to

    d) an invitation that elicits that friend's support and a contribution; and

    e) the link to your campaign.

2. Staying Ahead of the Curve — Discover one new social media platform. It could be one that only few people know about, or one that is starting to build up steam. It could be a photo-sharing site, a broadcast app, or something entirely new. Make sure it's a platform that you'll be able to utilize for your indie film and campaign. Once you find this platform, set up an account, learn how to use it, and start using it.

PART
6

ADVANCED
CROWDFUNDING

Chapter Thirty-Three

• • •

FROM LAO TZU TO SUN TZU: WAGING THE WAR OF ART

SO FAR, WE'VE gone down the list from crowdfunding basics to social media marketing for your film's campaign. We've even worked in some major tenets of Taoism, demonstrating how, by going with the flow of crowdfunding, your campaign will thrive; how through *Tao* you can set your campaign up with a strong team, the right platform, a smart strategy, and sufficient time to meet and possibly exceed your goal; how through *Te* you'll be able to show to your potential contributors an intimate part of you and your film in your invitation video, incentives, and social interactions; how your community can help you shape the *Pu* of your campaign and carry it toward the finish line; and how the principle of *wu wei* means that you have to get social to make the "ten thousand things," or $10,000 in this case, flow toward you without overdoing your efforts.

These precepts of Taoism are exemplary for launching a successful campaign for your film if you're looking to raise as little as a few hundred dollars to as much as $50,000. You may even be able to secure as much as $70,000 or $90,000. But for a feature-length film that might be budgeted up to around $100,000 or even $1M? For that, you'll need to temporarily close the *Tao Te Ching* and unlock the more proactive advice found in one of the world's oldest books on military strategy: Sun Tzu's *The Art of War*.

While everything you've learned about Lao Tzu's Taoist tome should still be applied to a crowdfunding campaign attempting to raise $100,000 or more, to even get close to that amount, you'll have to be a bit more active than the Taoist principle of *wu wei* dictates. You may need to crowdfund for a full two months rather than a few weeks. You may need to lure in larger contributions from individuals and investors behind the scenes looking to build a reputation in the industry as executive or associate producers by giving them further incentives for backing. You may also need to think about the bigger picture with regard to your film, like getting serious press, hiring a campaign manager, and securing distribution opportunities *before* your campaign is even live.

Doing this will require running your campaign much the same way an army general might run his campaign, with more strict regimentation than usual. That's where Sun Tzu's war-waging handbook comes into play. In the next chapters, I'll be making a few references to select sections of *The Art of War* that demonstrate how we as crowdfunders have to rethink the *Tao* of crowdfunding to counterbalance our efforts toward more ambitious fundraising targets, and maybe even come out with more than we thought we would once those goals are achieved.

Chapter Thirty-Four

...

$100K – $1M+ GOALS — HOW DO THEY RAISE IT?

SINCE MY EXPERIENCE with *Cerise*, indie filmmakers have been crowdfunding everything from the $10,000 thesis film to the $50,000 documentary. There have also been plenty of seasoned filmmakers who have raised more staggering amounts for their films: Malcolm Carter's *The Connected Universe*, which took home $258,250 from 2,791 people who believe in the interconnectedness of all things; *Black Angel*, the legendary short film that played before *The Empire Strikes Back* in 1980, will be getting a feature-length version thanks to 655 people helping director Roger Christian raise over $145,000 in sixty days; and Timo Vuorensola, the man who landed Nazis on the moon in the sci-fi comedy *Iron Sky* got a sequel written and a promo shot for $182,557 raised on Indiegogo by 3,517 backers, and then got *Iron Sky: The Coming Race* into production with over $600,000 raised between their second campaign (112% funded on Timo's $500,000 goal) and Indiegogo's InDemand, which keeps the page open to continue collecting funds after a successful campaign hits its deadline.

Then there are the (multi)million-dollar babies: Rob Thomas' *Veronica Mars* ($5.7M from 91,585 backers), Broken Lizard's *Super Troopers 2* ($4.5M from more than 51,000 backers), *Con Man* ($3.2M from 47,000 funders), Zach Braff's *Wish I Was Here* ($3.1M from 46,520 backers), *Blue Mountain State* ($1.9M from nearly 24,000 backers), and Spike Lee's "Newest Hottest Spike Lee Joint" *Da Sweet Blood of Jesus* ($1.4M from 6,421 backers).

I won't be discussing these campaigns in much more depth because the secret to their success is apparent, and if you think I'm going to say it's because they're "celebrity campaigns," you're mistaken. Of course, that *is* part of it, but the reason for their celebrity is because they've spent years doing the number one thing I mention throughout this book: *Build an audience first.* The fact is that if you spend over twelve years building up a rabid fan base because of the quality of the content you put out, you'll be able to raise $3.2M in crowdfunding too.

At the time of this writing, however, multimillion dollar campaigns are few and far between, so we'll be looking more deeply at campaigns that have raised amounts in the hundreds of thousands. For these kinds of film campaigns that require a little more bucks to get the right bang, you should take everything we've previously learned and amplify it with additional elements. The ancient Chinese militarist Sun Tzu was all about prowess and playing the war game smartly. Raising $100K to $1M or more is a war for your art. At this level, your focus is on laying plans and executing them, because the life of your film hangs in the balance.

Examining the plans of attack of a handful of crowdfunding campaigns that have garnered much praise for their strategies in reaching those heftier goals, here are a handful of things "you gotta have" in place *before* marching onto the battlefield.

YOU GOTTA HAVE AN AUDIENCE

While it is true that during your crowdfunding campaign you will be building your audience at the same time, when you're looking to raise substantial amounts of funding, it helps to already have an established base of fans for your indie film in place *before* launch.

It wasn't just the first *Iron Sky* movie that helped Timo and his producer Tero Kaukomaa erect a cult following that was partly responsible for not one, but two successful $100,000+ campaigns for *Iron Sky: The Coming Race*. Prior to that, Timo earned Internet fame in 1992 with the *Star Wreck* movies, a series of *Star Trek* parody films. In 1997, *Star Wreck V: Lost Contact* became the first near-feature-length film to be released to the public online for free.

Range 15 is another campaign that had a built-in audience before it launched its $325,000 Indiegogo, of which it raised over $1M between their campaign and InDemand. The military veterans who ran the campaign didn't just have the passion it takes to make a movie "so hardcore military it makes Hollywood wet itself and run home crying to Mommy"; they had the tactical ability to run it smartly. The reason they were able to raise over $874,000 during their deadline crowdfunding from nearly 8,000 fans was because they tapped into the military audience in two very big and strategic ways: First, they are veterans themselves, and second, they own the two biggest suppliers of military clothing in the world — Ranger Up and Article 15 Clothing — and the thousands of email addresses that helped make them the two biggest suppliers. On top of that, they have a YouTube channel with a subscriber base of nearly 50,000.

The power of the crowd should be harnessed as early on as possible, and the *Range 15* filmmakers built up their army and deployed their troops through a well-strategized Indiegogo campaign so they could make a military movie unlike any Hollywood has ever seen, and over 300% independent.

You Gotta Have a Gimmick

The word "gimmick" tends to get a bad rap. People who sense a gimmick usually back away from a person who's got one. They have a misconception about the word and often confuse it with the word "catch," as in the phrase, "What's the catch?" But a gimmick is really something that calls attention to something specific, like a particular perk or an overarching theme that you're playing up to the nth degree. If you're crowdfunding for a film in the hopes of raising $100,000 or more, you're going to need something more than hope and hard work — you're going to *need* a gimmick.

Take the Kickstarter for *Nintendo Quest*, which uses the concept of nostalgia as a gimmick. But the gimmick shouldn't stop at the theme alone; it needs to work its way through as many facets of the campaign as possible. For instance, one of the rewards that stood out most was the 8-bit soundtrack for *Nintendo Quest* — on cassette tape. Nothing spells nostalgia like offering a relic like this as a reward.

33.1. *The* Nintendo Quest *Official 8-Bit Soundtrack by John H. McCarthy is even more retro because it's on cassette.*

The Indiegogo to get merchandise manufactured for the genre film *Turbo Kid*, a story of a kid in a postapocalyptic 1997 who uses an ancient turbocharged weapon to defeat the baddies and save the girl of his dreams, offered similar 1990s nostalgic items, like a View-Master. They even offered the film itself in various forms, from VHS cassette to laser disc.

Another example of a more natural gimmick is Jennifer Fox's campaign for her feature-length documentary *My Reincarnation* about a Tibetan Buddhist master and his son as they tour the world, which raised $150,456 on Kickstarter. Its gimmick is that *My Reincarnation* is "an epic twenty-year journey," and Jennifer herself had been filming for two decades, as she made sure to mention in her description on Kickstarter:

> *My Reincarnation* has been a 20-year journey. For two decades I have filmed the esteemed Tibetan Buddhist master, Chögyal Namkhai Norbu, and his son, Khyentse Yeshe, around the world, from Italy to Venezuela, from Russia to Tibet and back again. This film is a never-before-seen insider's look at the passing of spiritual knowledge from a Tibetan Master to his Western-born son. It is a positive story of cultural transplantation, adaptation, and renewal that gives hope for the future of Tibetan culture in exile.

Again, the question becomes how someone like Jennifer who, in this case, wants to try to raise only $50,000, ends up raising triple that amount with subject matter that may not necessarily appeal to the general audience. One answer is that Jennifer kept up the "twenty years" aspect, which shows potential backers that this project is obviously important, interesting, and inspiring to her as a filmmaker and person. The other being that Jennifer also tapped into the right community and audience for the film.

"You Gotta Have Friends"

This is one of the truest lines I've ever heard in a James Cagney film: "I've learned that nobody can do much without somebody else," Paddy Ryan explains to Tom Powers and Matt Doyle in *The Public Enemy*. "Remember this boys, you gotta have friends." We all know this, that in just about every industry you can think of, you need to have friends who'll put in a good word for you and get you to the next level. The indie filmmaking industry is no exception, especially where crowdfunding is concerned.

But the kind of "friends" I'm talking about here is your actual family and close friends, because they are the ones you can rely on most. You should be able to gather from them the first 30% of your funding goal, and you should be able to do this within the first few days of your campaign. That said, if your crowdfunding goal is set at $150,000, then that first $45,000 needs to come from them, and they should make their contributions in the opening days. The reason is simple: Momentum. It's a long road to $150,000, and the general public, even those who really want to see your movie, will want to know that they're funding a winning campaign. You want to be able to sustain a steady flow of funds into your campaign, and starting strong is the best way to assure this momentum right out of the gate.

Think of yourself as a restaurateur getting your latest bistro ready for its grand opening. You've got to make sure that there are customers in the Indiegogo Café or Kickstart Diner on opening night, because no one likes to eat at an empty restaurant the first time the neon sign's turned on. It's up to us as campaigning filmmakers to make sure we have people sitting by the windows, to further entice passersby to take a peek at the décor (story) and menu (incentives) and decide to dine with us because other people are, too, and business is booming.

A prime difference between raising $25,000 and raising $100,000 rests on the concept of *confidence* versus *hard commitments*. If you're looking to get $25,000 and you're confident that your family and friends can get you that initial $7,500 in the first three days, then that's sufficient. When you're raising $100,000 and up, however, and you're relying on those same family members and friends to get you the first third, confidence is a good start, but hard commitments are smart, and "soft launching," or launching early to only your friends, family members, and diehard supporters to obtain those commitments, is even smarter. (Don't worry, we'll talk more about soft launching your film campaign in Chapter Thirty-Seven.)

You Gotta Have Patience

As any crowdfunder will tell you, much of the experience of crowdfunding is trial and error. There is really no one right way to crowdfund, though there are a few not-so-right ways, and when things don't go according to plan, patience should be exercised. I brought up things like the lull earlier, those times when it's difficult to push on, which happens to just about every campaign, whether the end goal is $15,000 or $50,000. But at $100,000 and up, patience becomes more than a virtue; it becomes a necessity if your campaign is to survive.

Even if you're not using a crowdfunding platform and are going about fundraising on your own website, once you start your campaign, it will no doubt take a little bit of time to build up momentum. Again, a great example is Antony D. Lane's *Invasion of the Not Quite Dead*. Through a handful of Tweetathons, he managed to raise a staggering amount of money, and when I was tweeting with him one day, he confessed that "the Twitter community have been BEYOND amazing, although after thirty months, it's taken PATIENCE."

Sun Tzu states in Chapter Two of *The Art of War* that, "if victory is long in coming, then men's weapons will grow dull and their ardor will be damped." It's difficult even for me to see so many tweets about this particular film, but if there's one thing Lane's got aside from patience, it's perseverance. The bulk of us are happy to call it quits after two months of crowdfunding, especially if our campaigns get caught in the lull and find no way out. But Lane's weapons surely haven't dulled, and his ardor for his project has not dampened. An anomaly for sure, but one we can all learn something from.

YOU GOTTA HAVE FUN

Yes, crowdfunding is a full-time job. Yes, you won't sleep much. Yes, you may become slightly malnourished. And yes, you may do all of this and not reach your goal. Multiply this exponentially by the size of your end goal, and you might want to turn away from crowdfunding altogether, get a second or third job, and raise the money that way. Despite all of this, crowdfunding can and should be enjoyable, and most of the time that fun starts with your invitation and follows through all the way to your incentives, interactions, and beyond.

It's no secret that most people like to laugh, especially when watching movies and videos, so when you're putting together your campaign video, try to make them laugh, or at the very least cause them to crack a smile. It doesn't matter if your film is a stoner comedy or as serious in subject matter as Jocelyn Towne's *I Am I*. This movie tells the story of a young woman whose estranged father's mental illness convinces him that she's not his daughter, but his deceased wife. When the girl decides to play along, she begins "to discover the truth about her parents' past and these revelations shed a new light on the present."

The video for *I Am I*, however, is very light and talks nothing about the film itself, but rather how Jocelyn went about getting from script to look book to crowdfunding. From producers popping up from behind her couch and her interrupting her actor-husband in the bathtub to ask if he'd play the lead role to inviting friends and random strangers into their bed as a metaphor for how awkward crowdfunding is ("like asking someone to go to bed with you"), I couldn't help but laugh out loud more than once. At the same time, I also got a sense of how important this story is for Jocelyn, and I saw her passion through the duration of her invitation video. Most importantly, I saw lots of people having fun, and who wouldn't give money to something fun?

Crowdfunding is serious business, yes, but it doesn't have to *feel* so serious. It's okay to have a good time with your team and your contributors.

You Gotta Have *Two* Stories

You may love the story that you want to tell in the film you're crowdfunding, but to think that everyone will want to hear that story is somewhat unrealistic. We live in a society of niche films, which is a plus since nowadays any and every film that is made will have an audience. But with crowdfunding, you may not want to simply rely on a niche audience. The ultimate question is how do you get someone who doesn't care about sports movies or films that are spiritual in nature to care about and support your film? Easy. You give them another story to be inspired by: *your* story.

This doesn't necessarily mean you should tell people all the intricate details of how you discovered your love of film shooting videos with your high school buddies, which is a bit cliché nowadays. You should tell the story that revolves around the film for which you want to raise these considerable funds. By doing so, you also address the urgency of the situation and answer the question most people will be asking themselves: "Why should I contribute to this film campaign *right now*?"

A prime example of this is Steve Taylor's film adaptation of author Donald Miller's bestselling book *Blue Like Jazz*, a story about "non-religious thoughts on Christian spirituality." The campaign was set up by two fans, Zach Prichard and Jonathan Frazier, with the goal of raising $125,000, the amount needed to make this film. Originally, *Blue Like Jazz* had two investors at $250,000 each. Then one of them dropped out at the start of preproduction. Not getting too into the "sob" element of this story, Zach and Jonathan's campaign video simply states that "Don announced on his blog that despite a strong screenplay, a stellar cast, and rave

179

reviews, the film would be on hold indefinitely, simply because there was not enough funding."

Then, a giant question mark appears on screen, and with disapproval scratching his voice, Zach poses the ludicrous truth in question, that "they aren't going to make this film because of funding?!" Because of this impressive campaign, Zach and Jonathan brought in a whopping $345,992 with the help of almost 4,495 backers on Kickstarter. What was their focus? Simply put, the absurdity of a film, with a story they and many others believed was worth telling, not being made simply because of a lack of funding. That alone became the anchor that grounded *Blue Like Jazz* in the hearts of almost 4,500 backers and helped this massively successful campaign toward amazing new heights and record dollar amounts.

YOU GOTTA HAVE GUTS

Crowdfunding for films like *Blue Like Jazz*, *I Am I*, *My Reincarnation*, and *Iron Sky: The Coming Race* takes lots of time, strategy, and plenty of patience and perseverance, but it also requires the courage to shout to the world, "I need $100,000 to make my film, and I believe that *you* will give it to me." The minute you think of the other side of the crowdfunding coin — that you might not raise that money — it's over before it's even begun. And with crowdfunding, you not only fail, but you fail in plain sight of everyone you know — your family, your friends, and your social networks.

It was because of doubt and fear that I almost didn't launch my campaign for *Cerise*, and that was for only $5,000. At this much larger scale, when the fear factor rises, your self-confidence will freeze up, but we simply can't allow this type of internal paralysis to set in. Yes, let the fear in, but as Jack Shephard says in the opening episode of *Lost*, only let the fear in for five seconds, and then get to work.

Remember, crowdfunding isn't about the money, and it's not about us filmmakers, either. It's about the movies we're trying to fund, movies that could be seen by hundreds, perhaps thousands of people worldwide once they're finished; movies that could change lives, make people think differently about certain issues and topics, cause them to see the world, or at the very least their respective worlds, in a different light. If we allow our egos to override this crowdfunding truth, then our movies benefit no one.

Perhaps Jennifer Fox worded it best in an interview she had with Indiewire:

> "Announcing to all the world on the Internet that my film had a deficit was the most naked thing I have ever done," Fox said in a statement. "In the past, I always approached fundraising as a private hush-hush event. Going public really shook up my egotistical concepts of who I was as a person. I started to reflect on that in my blog posts in a way that related to the film's spiritual content."

It doesn't take guts to fail, but it takes guts to succeed. Contributors may be drawn to give to your campaign by the sheer force or your personality or past accomplishments. Your drive in crowd-funding for your film, however, should not be about you but about the message you're trying to get out into the world — your ideas married to your contributors' support. And yes, it takes guts to send out that first email, tweet, and Facebook update, and that courage must stay strong and steady from launch to success.

Chapter Thirty-Five

...

WHEN TO BRING ON A CAMPAIGN MANAGER

CROWDFUNDING FOR INDEPENDENT film has grown up quite a bit since the first edition of *Crowdfunding for Filmmakers*, and as such, those who partake in the privilege that is inviting a crowd in to fund your latest movie must adapt to the changing landscape. As Pearl Jam's Eddie Vedder sings, "It's evolution, baby!" and one such evolution has been the advent of the *campaign manager*.

Yes, crowdfunding is a booming industry, one that has spawned an ecosystem all its own: people who have made it their jobs to handle every facet of your campaign for you. They strategize the campaign trail, organize the assets, secure exclusives and other press, schedule social media outreach, set up interviews, post updates to the campaign, and oftentimes work with you up until the campaign has fulfilled its incentives to make sure your backers have had a Grade A experience with the campaign.

In terms of fees, campaign managers typically take a retainer up front and a percentage of the total funds raised in the campaign as payment. And as you might well imagine, this is quite a lucrative business because, after all, crowdfunding is a full-time job, and if you don't have the time to make campaigning your nine-to-five, you hire someone who can.

The fact is that the majority of campaigns that raise $100,000, and especially the $1M ones, are completely run by campaign managers. No, director Rob Thomas did not run the *Veronica Mars* Kickstarter; Wil Wheaton was the face of the Indiegogo for season three of his hit YouTube gaming series *TableTop*, but he wasn't the one pulling the strings making things happen from day one to almost triple the campaign's $500,000 goal; and Alan Tudyk and Nathan Fillion were able to do press and promote their Indiegogo for *Con Man* because there was a campaign manager working diligently behind the scenes keeping this multimillion dollar web series running smoothly. There are even some film campaigns out that have entire agencies working on various aspects of their campaigns.

There are others, however, that do extremely well without a campaign manager on board, like the Indiegogo campaign for Don Bluth and Gary Goldman's *Dragon's Lair*, an animated movie based on the groundbreaking video game from the 1980s that introduced gamers to 2-D animated gameplay. Don and Gary had originally launched a Kickstarter for $550,000, which they discovered needed a reset shortly after launch because of their overpriced rewards and little knowledge of what crowdfunding can and cannot do for indie film. They switched to Indiegogo, listened to their fans, and worked very closely with me to help strategize the *Dragon's Lair* Returns campaign. By setting a more modest goal of $250,000 and being open to putting in the full-time work a campaign demands, they were able to hit that target quickly and continue journeying past their original Kickstarter goal of $550,000 with Indiegogo's InDemand.

The real question is when should you, as an independent filmmaker, bring on a campaign manager? And what should you look for in one? Let's start backward: Here are a few things you should look for in a campaign manager:

A Proven Track Record

When searching for a campaign manager, you want to find one who has some sort of a track record. That doesn't mean if you're looking to raise $100,000 for your film and you meet with a campaign manager who's never had a campaign raise more than $60,000 that you shouldn't entertain him or her with an interview. Remember, many campaign managers are still starting out, and raising $60,000 is still a lot of money.

LOGIC. CREATIVITY. HUSTLE.

Crowdfunding is something that all campaign managers are still figuring out as they go along, and anyone who says different is just protecting his or her ego. I learn something new with every campaign I work with at Indiegogo.

A good campaign manager (and I am *very* particular with what I consider "good" with regard to campaign managers) should have a solid foundation in traditional fundraising while at the same time being on top of the trends for making crowdfunding easier for the campaigner and more enjoyable for the potential contributors.

He or she should be well versed in Amanda Palmer's *Art of Asking* and the craft of Gary Vaynerchuk's *Crush It!* and hold firmly to Tony Hsieh's sensitivity to *Delivering Happiness*. A potential campaign manager should be one part logistical, one part creative, and all hustle. He or she should understand the basics of digital marketing (Facebook ads and promoted posts, Google AdWords, and other forms of digital advertising), especially for campaigns looking to raise $500,000 and up, since without some money spent on digital marketing, you can't expect to hit those high amounts organically through simple social media outreach.

If your candidate doesn't have all of these qualities, that's fine. But a potential campaign manager should at least have the sense to hire people who do have the tools he or she may be lacking, to best serve you and your film campaign.

The Ability to Build Your Audience

It's one thing if you can find a campaign manager who can help you raise the $100,000 to $1M you're looking to make your movie with, but it's another thing to be able to raise an audience that has awareness of your film. A good campaign manager should be able to do both. Remember, the crowd must always come before the funding; a $200,000 raise from 8,000 people is much more impressive than $1M from 1,500 because it's a more accurate barometer of how much support your indie film actually has from the crowd.

That said, you should always make sure that the campaign manager you're looking to hire has a plan for getting you more exposure without relying on their crowdfunding platform of choice or the indie film's built-in audience. I worked with a particular campaign manager on a few film campaigns. One of the films had a built-in audience, so it was fairly easy for the manager to create interesting content and engage with that audience through good content and constant updates. During another campaign, one that didn't have any kind of built-in audience, this same campaign manager was not able to discover and deliver that audience for the filmmakers because building an audience from scratch is very different from interacting with one that's full of ardent fans already sold on the film.

Consultants vs. Managers — What's the Difference?

What's the difference between a crowdfunding consultant and a campaign manager? Simple: The consultant advises you on best practices and, at times, will give direct feedback on your campaign page, video, incentives, and overall strategy. What he or she won't do is run the campaign for you. The campaign manager, on the other hand, will do all that *and* run the campaign.

Back to the first question: When should you bring on a campaign manager? If you do have the time to run your own crowdfunding campaign for your indie film, then perhaps all you may need is a consultation with someone who understands the landscape of crowdfunding for film and who can help you come up with some ideas for your particular campaign — be it some unique 3-D! incentives or an interesting way to format your invitation video to best serve your audience and stand out from other film campaigns — which you can then implement yourself. But if you really need the help of another person who's trained in the art and craft of online fundraising for independent film, then bringing on a campaign manager is probably the best choice you can make for your film.

· · ·

Chapter Thirty-Six

Fiscal Sponsorships, Matching Funds, and Equity: Added Incentive for Contributors

Sometimes a highly personalized invitation video just isn't enough to coax a person to click the "Contribute Now" button. Sometimes incentives as unique and interesting as the film itself fall shy of making someone reach for his or her Visa or MasterCard. Sometimes, even tons of fun interactions, quirky promotion, and other campaign updates and a well-thought-out marketing strategy just won't make someone become a contributor to your film at anything more than the $10 or $25 level. And at those times, and especially if you're looking to raise six figures or more, you may need to entice funders with financial incentives, rather than just the perks and rewards you're currently offering.

Fiscal Sponsorship

Fiscal sponsorship gives potential backers the ability to contribute to your campaign and write it off as a donation on their tax forms. By partnering up with a nonprofit organization like Fractured Atlas and other filmmaker-friendly groups, crowdfunders can offer their contributors the added incentive of a charitable deduction for income tax purposes, a service that, individually, they would not be able to offer. Indiegogo has very strong partnerships with Fractured Atlas ($11.5M raised between nearly 2,500 campaigns) and From the Heart Productions ($1.9M raised by over 320 campaigns). The two have been helping filmmakers reach their crowdfunding goals since 2010 and 2011, respectively.

So what exactly are Fractured Atlas and other organizations like it? Rather than try to explain this, I'll let Fractured Atlas give it to you in the simplest of terms:

> With fiscal sponsorship, you can solicit tax-deductible donations and apply for grants without going through the onerous process of launching a 501(c)(3). The sponsored "project" might be a one-time collaboration or an independent artist or even an arts organization that does not have its own 501(c)(3) status.

A more detailed description of what fiscal sponsorship is and how it works can be found on Fractured Atlas' website, along with more information about how its partnership with Indiegogo and other crowdfunding platforms work. But what are the added incentives for you, the crowdfunder, for going the fiscal sponsorship route over using your crowdfunding platform alone? For starters, on Indiegogo, there is a set fee of 7% charged to campaigns connected to Fractured Atlas, which includes the platform *and* credit card fees, so by the end of your indie film campaign you will end up paying less of your earnings to Indiegogo and the credit card companies.

Another incentive for you as a crowdfunder, which is briefly mentioned in the above description, is that Fractured Atlas also gives you access to foundation and government grants that may only be accessible to nonprofit organizations or fiscally sponsored projects. This means that you can raise some money through crowdfunding, which will also give you an early opportunity to build a following and a fan base for when your film is finished. You can also take the more traditional route and try to obtain grants and scholarships, which may ultimately give you even more funding to work with on your film in the long run, and if you run a successful crowdfunding campaign, of course.

Again, there is much more detailed information available on Fractured Atlas' website (*www.fracturedatlas.org*), so you can read up on the inner workings of fiscal sponsorship and decide whether it would be a good option for your film campaign.

MATCHING FUNDS

Another tactic that can be used at any time during a campaign is *matching funds*, in which a person or organization offers to match dollar-for-dollar what contributors give to your film campaign up to a certain amount. This way, if a potential backer knows that during a particular time — it could be twenty-four hours or a week — if they contribute $25, it's matched, they can feel great knowing that their contribution was really worth $50 for the campaign because of the match.

This is a tactic that has been used for decades by many organizations, most notably by public radio stations during their membership drives. I'm a fan of WFUV, a public radio station that's run out of Fordham University in New York, and after many years listening to shows like *The Alternate Side*, *Group Harmony Review*, and *The Big Broadcast*, I finally became a proud member with a $60 contribution. However, at the time of my pledge, there was a matching funds drive happening, so my $60 contribution for the year was worth $120, and I felt even better knowing that every dollar I contributed went twice as far.

As with anything that pertains to crowdfunding an indie film, I always recommend setting these kinds of strategies up in advance of the campaign's launch, or at the very least getting the process started, because sometimes there are legalities that need a bit of ironing out before an organization can come on board and officially offer matching funds for a campaign.

EQUITY CROWDFUNDING

Then there's *equity crowdfunding*, specifically the JOBS (Jumpstart Our Business Startups) Act, signed into law by President Obama in 2012. This legislation makes it possible for investors to invest equity into small businesses via the Internet in an attempt to jumpstart the American economy and create new jobs and a more financially stable country. What does this mean for crowdfunders of short and feature-length films? You will now be able to offer a return on investment to anyone who comes on board as an equity investor. Instead of offering those backers the T-shirt or merch-based incentives in exchange for their $50 or $100 contribution, you can offer something more appealing to an investor: a share in your film's profits.

Currently, equity crowdfunding is strictly being developed for business startups, but because the law revolves specifically around the concept of crowdfunding, it will ultimately affect all facets of online fundraising, from small startups to short films. And although equity crowdfunding is still fairly new in the US, it has been around for quite some time in other countries, namely the United Kingdom. In fact, at the time of this writing, there have been two films crowdfunded on a very modest scale using equity as an incentive for investors to make the films happen: one is *Con Air* director Simon West's film *Salty*, using equity crowdfunding platform SyndicateRoom, raising £2.2M; the other director Lee Tamahori's film *The Patriarch*, which raised $488,800 from 204 investors on the New Zealand–based equity crowdfunding platform Snowball Effect.

Ever since the Securities and Exchange Commission (SEC) firmed up procedures for properly governing online fundraising back in October of 2015, industry experts, business lawyers, and crowd leaders have been posting content about Title II and Title III of the JOBS Act, which concern themselves with equity and debt crowdfunding, and Regulation A+, which, according to crowdfunding attorney Mark Roderick, "allows issuers to raise up to $50 million per year from both accredited and non-accredited investors."

Equity crowdfunding is the natural evolution of its rewards-based brethren, and being as serious a business as making movies the traditional way has always been, there are those who are for it and those who are against it. Some would caution filmmakers to "avoid Reg A+ like the plague" like entertainment finance attorney David Pierce, and others will laud its greatness because of its ability to turn movie lovers into movie investors. One thing is for sure, though: Do *your* homework and research every aspect of equity crowdfunding so you understand *exactly* what you're getting into as a filmmaker. There's a huge difference between accepting a $50,000 investment and taking a $50 contribution.

That said, I recommend keeping a close eye on the rapidly changing landscapes of both perks-based and equity crowdfunding. There are many organizations out there, from the CrowdFund Intermediary Regulatory Advocates (CFIRA) to the Crowdfunding Professional Association (CfPA), but two trustworthy sites you should subscribe to are Crowdfund Insider (*http://crowdfundinsider.com*) and The National Crowdfunding Association (*http://nlcfa.org*), and/or follow them on Twitter (@CrowdfundInside and @NLCFA, respectively), to keep in the know so you can make the best decision as to which kind of crowdfunding is right for your particular film.

Chapter Thirty-Seven

• • •

SOFT LAUNCHES, PRE-LAUNCH CAMPAIGNS, AND STRETCH GOALS: PROVEN STRATEGIES FOR SUCCESS

LIKE MY FRIEND Princeton who ran an unsuccessful crowdfunding campaign mentions in the guest post he wrote for Film Courage, sometimes "Twitter & Facebook alone will NOT get your film funded on Kickstarter or Indiegogo." That said, whether you're trying to raise $10,000, like he was, or $500,000 for your ambitious feature-length movie, most times you may not be able to rely solely on setting up a stellar campaign, launching it, and then waiting to see how it's received. Success at this level is the result of planning, preparation, and diligence in its execution.

The following are strategies that most successful film campaigners have used to make certain that their films are not only fully funded, but oftentimes overfunded by more contributions from more backers than they ever thought possible.

SOFT LAUNCHING FOR A SMART START

You might be asking yourself, "What's the difference between a soft and regular launch?" Starting in reverse, a regular or an "official" launch, is the one that happens the day you send out the first email to your contact list, the first tweet and Facebook update about your film campaign to your extended network. A *soft launch* is the more intimate launch that precedes it, hyper-targeted toward getting family members, close friends, extended relatives, and even prior supporters to become the first *core contributors* of your campaign.

The way a soft launch should run is twofold. First, in a brief personalized email to this *host committee* of core contributors, explain to them that you're about to launch a crowdfunding campaign, and that you:

- are thankful for all the support they've shown over the years and

- would love for them to be among your first supporters to your campaign, which

- will be launching on *x* date.

Notice anything strange here? There is no mention of "money," "funding," or "contributing" in this initial message. The focus here is to let them know you're going to run a campaign and that you'd appreciate their support at the start. This is also for you to gauge how much of those hard commitments I mentioned in Chapter Thirty-Four you can get to secure the first third of your funding. That's it. Send it.

Next, after about three days or a week or so, send them the follow-up email. This is where we rack focus on *how* they can support, which is to contribute, so be sure to:

- set a hard deadline for them to contribute by (within three days is best), and

- reiterate how important it is that they get involved first, and also

- ask them to spread the word about your campaign *after* they've contributed.

Notice anything equally as strange? This email revolves around support, but financial *and* social, not financial *or* social. You wouldn't want to leave the choice to fund *or* to share with them, because most folks will probably choose the option that costs them less. You should invite them to do both, and in this way, when you officially launch your film campaign, those who visit will see you've already got a good chunk of funding and support, which builds credibility and shows the crowd to come that your film just may be worth putting their faith *and* their funds into.

PREFUNDIA, THUNDERCLAP, AND GREEN INBOX

Audience building proves very difficult to most filmmakers, so *amplification* is something that has become more and more important in crowdfunding an independent film, since every filmmaker wants his or her movie seen by as many people as possible. This need has spawned online and mobile services that aid in the amplification process, sometimes before the campaign goes live, and in other instances right at the moment of launch.

Take Prefundia and Thunderclap, for example, two platforms that offer pre-launch services to help you build your audience and message them on the day of your film campaign's launch. With Prefundia (and Indiegogo as well), you can set up a "coming soon" page and start spreading the word about your campaign before launch. The cool thing here is that it enables you to interact with your crowd to get feedback on your project, which is essentially crowdsourcing a stronger Indiegogo or Kickstarter. The main feature of a coming soon page, however, is a seemingly simple one, but so very important: It allows visitors interested in the film and campaign to opt in via email for an early invite to your campaign once it launches. Getting email addresses is becoming increasingly more difficult. With a pre-launch page, it's just a little easier.

Thunderclap amplifies — or *explodes*, as they describe it — whatever message you want to get across by having supporters blast out your message en masse to their followers and friends. Billed as a "crowd-speaking" platform, Thunderclap is not only used for crowdfunding, but also for any message that you'd like to gather people together for and push out a call to action as widely as possible, all at once, which is the main draw. A successful Thunderclap involves reaching a target number of supporters, which calculates a "social reach" based on those supporters' social media followings. Then, on the day of the deadline, every person who "joined the Thunder" will share their customizable messages about the film at the same exact time to their followers.

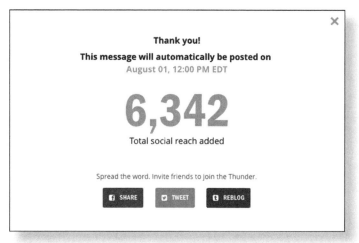

37.1. *This Thunderclap campaign was shared to a "social reach" of over 6,000 people.*

Now, Green Inbox is an interesting case. How it works is that it connects with your Facebook friends directly via email so that you can send your entire friends list, or a subset of that list, the same message. Essentially, it's like a mail merge for Facebook, and this works since the trouble with Facebook is that if you want to personally send messages to all of your friends, there's no way to do that in one shot. More importantly, once you hit a certain limit, Facebook flags you for spam and freezes your Facebook page. Green Inbox, therefore, is a way around this.

While I can't necessarily recommend using Green Inbox, one can't deny the case studies and data that show that this method does, in fact, work for many campaigns, like the Indiegogo for the web series *Hollywood Beauty Detective*. Series creator Holly Fulger states on the site that she raised $10,000 of that as a direct result of Green Inbox. And though Holly's campaign raised a total of $25,580 and not $100,000 or more, on a larger campaign, that $10,000 right out of the gate, combined with your host committee contributions, can push you well over the 30% threshold. This will certainly create an intense momentum that can be more easily sustained throughout the campaign.

Now, much the way I wouldn't recommend using an email service like MailChimp or Constant Contact for your initial outreach to actual friends of yours, the same goes for Green Inbox. Those people deserve to be invited to join your campaign through personal emails or Facebook messages. For all of your remaining Facebook friends, Green Inbox should prove a very useful tool.

Keep in mind, however, that Green Inbox is a paid service. Prices vary from Facebook, LinkedIn, and Twitter direct messages to email and phone services; there's even a slightly more expensive option that outreaches to bloggers and websites that have written about crowdfunding campaigns in the past, too. If you're looking to raise $100,000 or more, you probably have a budget to spend on marketing, and according to the testimonials, a modest investment in Green Inbox may yield a massive payout.

STRETCH GOALS (OR, HOW TO GET FROM $100K TO $1M)

You've hit your crowdfunding goal, and you take a few minutes to celebrate this immense victory and realization that, thanks to all these amazing backers of your film campaign, you will now be able to make an awesome film.

But then you look at your ending date and realize that you've still got two weeks left before the campaign closes! Do you stop? Do you let the campaign sit there, fat-full of the funding you wanted? Of course not, although that's exactly what I did when I hit my goal for *Cerise* in two-thirds the length of the campaign. I let it sit on Indiegogo until the days remaining ticked down to zero, and in that time, $1,600 in additional funding came in without me sending a single email, tweet, or update.

Imagine if I had kept going? If I had set a *stretch goal* or two. If there were even such a thing as a stretch goal back then.

That was then, and this is now, and now, properly set stretch goals can earn filmmakers even more money for the films they're trying to get funded. A common mistake many filmmakers make is having the stretch goals be about their films when the focus needs to shift to the contributors and what *they* will get out of helping your film campaign hit subsequent goals. A few years ago, giving them a "better film" was sufficient enough a reason; nowadays it doesn't make the cut.

The biggest key to hitting your stretch goals is to be very realistic and clear with those stretch goals, particularly in terms of what you can do with the extra funds and what your contributors will get in return. I recommend outlining three distinct stretch goals visually on your campaign to let people know you're still raising funds beyond your initial goal. In terms of being realistic with these new targets, if your initial goal was $150,000, I recommend your first stretch goal be a modest one and relatively easy to achieve at $160,000. Because it's *only* $10,000 more, you'll quickly hit it. The second stretch goal could then strive a bit further at $180,000, and a final stretch goal could be set at $200,000, depending on how quickly you hit the previous goals.

The size of these stretch goals is also contingent on the size of your growing network of followers, fans, and backers. If you have a larger, more ardent network from which to draw, you can stretch those goals a bit further out. Take a look at the stretch goals set and surpassed by the campaigners behind the Indiegogo to bring back the hit 1990s television game show *The Crystal Maze*.

37.2. The team behind The Crystal Maze *made sure to design each aspect of their three "Completed!" stretch goals with a good time in mind.*

The campaign brought together over 6,700 passionate fans, young and old, to successfully earn the *Crystal Maze* team an astounding £927,252. That's 185% funded! Compare this to an equally successful stretch campaign for *Supernatural*'s Richard Speight Jr. and Rob Benedict's comedy web series *Kings of Con* (no relation to *Con Man*, though *uniquely* similar in premise) about what really makes comic cons crazy and unpredictable: the actors paid to attend! The duo set out to raise $100,000, which would enable them to produce three episodes. They set stretch goals to get them to the full slate — an additional $25,000 a piece — and they made it past the $250,000 stretch goal, but fell just $20,000 shy of funding the full season.

37.3. Creativity and value are key when unlocking new incentives to help the crowd help you reach your stretch goals.

The reason is simple enough to see: At each of the unlocked stretch goals, it became more about what *they* would be doing, which was another episode, plus special guest appearances, guest stars, a bonus teaser, and then at $300,000, "more GUEST STARS announced!" It got a little old, and there were no incentives for the fans to keep funding the series. Granted, Richard and Rob made it far, but had they offered more value to the fans, they might have surpassed $300,000.

This is why I always recommend "unlocking" a brand-new incentive — preferably something everyone who has already supported the campaign will get in addition to their selected perk or reward. If not this, then a new incentive that can be acquired as an upgrade for current backers or as a brand-new one for potential contributors. I got on board the *Nintendo Quest* Kickstarter once I saw that every backer at the $25 level would receive the 8-bit soundtrack on cassette. The bare-bones DVD was good enough at $25, but by surpassing their second stretch goal, the filmmakers were able to offer something that a lot of people couldn't turn down for the price.

A final stretch goal tactic that works wonders is offering *secret incentives* to a subset of your contributor base. You'll know the most ardent of your supporters when you see them. They're the ones tweeting voraciously about your campaign. Reach out to them directly and offer them a special reward on top of what they've already selected for an amount that's easily trackable amid 1,000 or more contributors ($11, $27, $42, etc.). This shows those backers that you are thankful for their help and also demonstrates how much you want to hit your stretch goals — by making it all about them. Indiegogo has made offering secret perks even simpler to offer with a feature that generates a link that will reveal the secret perk to only those who click that link.

The most important thing to remember is that it's called a *stretch* goal for a reason. Like a rubber band, you have to stretch out your goal gradually to earn that additional funding. The same way that yanking on a rubber band will cause it to snap, so will a stretch goal if you try to yank from your $100,000 initial goal to a lofty $500,000 stretch goal. The crowd will snip it with a pair of scissors before you even have the chance to yank it.

• Part Six •
Summary Points

- To raise \$100,000+ on Indiegogo or Kickstarter, you "gotta have" an audience, a gimmick, friends, patience, fun, two stories, and most importantly, guts.

- If you're bringing on a campaign manager to run your campaign, be sure he or she has a track record and will do more for you than a crowdfunding consultant would offer.

- Added incentives for contributions like fiscal sponsorship through a 501(c)(3) nonprofit organization and matching funds drives can help certain film campaigns raise more substantial amounts and reach their goals faster.

- Equity crowdfunding will soon become a viable option for film financing in the years to come, so keep up to date with as much as you can — mainly Title III and Title IV (Regulation A+) of the JOBS Act — to see if it is something you can use to fund your first bigger-budget indie films.

- Put together a host committee of your closest friends, family members, and supporters of your previous work. Soft launch to them in your campaign's opening days to build the proper momentum to sustain your campaign beyond your goal and into your stretch goals, where you can raise further funds.

- When setting stretch goals after you've hit your initial goal, always be realistic and clear about what you will do with those funds and what your potential contributors will get for helping you hit those additional targets.

• PART SIX •
EXERCISE

Think about your two stories — your personal story and indie film's synopsis. How can you combine the two to create a grander story? What are some ways you might work this larger story into various aspects of your campaign to help build a larger audience for and awareness of your film, its crowdfunding campaign, and you as a filmmaker?

PART
7

CROWD
STUDIES

• • •

THE [SMALLEST] SPACE BETWEEN FANS AND FUNDRAISING

I DECIDED TO start this section of crowd studies with Amy Jo Johnson's campaign for her feature-length film *The Space Between* for a very particular reason — it illustrates a fundamental part of crowdfunding that needs to be stated, restated, understood, and never brought up again: When we decide to crowdfund, we *must* place ourselves on the same level as the crowd, and we've got to give that crowd we're a part of 100% of our passion for our indie films in order for them to get us over 100% funded. In short, the space between a campaigner and his or her audience must be the smallest space possible, and Amy Jo's Indiegogo illustrates this in more ways than just a playful use of the title.

To the uninitiated, the campaign for *The Space Between* could be mistaken as a celebrity campaign (more about that in Trignosis #5) because if you do not know Amy Jo Johnson by name, if you grew up in the 1990s you'll certainly remember her as the Pink Ranger from the *Mighty Morphin Power Rangers* television series. But in the end, it was not because of Amy Jo's celebrity that she reached her crowdfunding goal of $75,000; it was a result of a lot of pre-launch preparation, nonstop hustle up until the end of her campaign, and plenty of fun throughout.

Also worth noting is that *The Space Between* is not Amy Jo's first film or her first crowdfunding campaign. Between 2012 and 2013, she crowdfunded two short films, one called *Bent*, for which she raised $28,832 on a $20,000 goal from 202 backers, and the other called *Lines*, which brought in $46,169 on a $25,000 target from

285 people. *The Space Between* does mark Amy Jo's first crowd-funded feature-length film.

PREPARATION BEFORE LAUNCH

I remember meeting Amy Jo and her producer Jessica Adams at Sense Appeal Coffee Shop on Spadina Avenue during the Toronto International Film Festival in 2013. We spoke at length about the potential her Indiegogo for *The Space Between* had to be yet another success story for Amy Jo and for Indiegogo. Since that day, they were in constant contact with me, and together we prepped the campaign.

But Amy Jo's preparation started much further back than that. Again, being the Pink Ranger got her international recognition and a pretty immense following in the tens of thousands on Twitter alone. Through her short films and her blossoming career as an independent writer and director, Amy Jo continued building her audience further out than even her previous prowess as a Power Ranger had allowed.

Part of this preparation was being sure she set a realistic goal. The main concern was that because Amy Jo had run two campaigns prior to the one she would launch for *The Space Between* she would be tapping into the same fan base — a fan base that most likely had already given her money for one or both short film campaigns. So Amy Jo had to manage her expectations and set a goal that she was 100% confident she could secure the first third of, and then, by unveiling perks ranging from signed headshots to *Power Ranger* props, as well as a plethora of other 3-D! incentives, secure the remaining funds needed for a successful Indiegogo experience.

NO SPACES LEFT EMPTY

Amy Jo's campaign was one of the first Indiegogo campaigns that I've worked with that really went above and beyond in terms of the look and feel of the campaign. From the layout and design of the story to all of the promotional materials, Amy Jo and her team didn't let anything go out to the public that wasn't professional. From Facebook cover photos to beautifully designed images like the one below beckoning potential contributors to "Contribute & Join the Team," everything was on brand, colorful, and a pleasure to look at.

38.1. *Eye-popping imagery like this Indiegogo-branded call to action from Amy Jo Johnson's* The Space Between *helped get fans to "join the team."*

It takes a bit more time to create images like this, but again, your crowdfunding campaign should strive to be an extension of the indie film you're looking to make, and today, images matter, even on websites that once were strictly text-based like Twitter; statistically, you'll get more clicks on your links if you have an eye-catching image accompanying them.

CONSTANT CONTACT *AND* CONTENT

From signed photographs in costume as the Pink Ranger to a surfeit of videos on her YouTube channel, Amy Jo was never at a loss for content, and content is king in crowdfunding an indie film. For instance, aside from her videos, she got a few of her fellow Rangers to create their own, daring her to busk on the streets of Toronto in a Pink Power Ranger costume if she hit her goal. Well, she hit her $75,000, and she took off to scour all the costume shops in Toronto searching for a Pink Power Ranger costume, and she took her entire audience with her, filming her looking through the racks in various stores.

Connecting with your backers in this way and letting them see beyond the metaphorical curtain opens you up to endless opportunities for generating content that you can share with that same audience. Perhaps you'll even get them to share with their friends and followers to help further build up your audience even more.

SOMETHING NOW, SOMETHING LATER

You may recall my mentioning back in Chapter Eighteen that you should offer some incentives that you can fulfill immediately and others, like the film in various forms, that you will fulfill later. Well, Amy Jo went above and beyond in this department, and she is certain that it had a huge impact on the success of her campaign:

> "I would do a twenty-four-hour sale. Anyone who donated in the next twenty-four hours got a personal video message. Other days it was personal voice messages. Then we would deliver these a few days later while the campaign was still running. It seemed to really bring in a ton of traffic every time we did this."

This brings us to another main lesson, which is the importance of those highly personalized 3-D! incentives I spoke about in

Chapter Fourteen. Amy Jo didn't cut any corners like many others who have her level of renown might. Her Indiegogo reached over $134,000 (and is still raising thanks to InDemand) from more than 1,460 backers because she offered her most ardent fans and followers as much of herself as she needed to get her to her initial goal, and she offered a lot.

What we can take out of how Amy Jo Johnson ran her Indiegogo for *The Space Between* is simple: *Run your indie film's crowdfunding campaign with your audience in mind*, from pre- to post-campaign, and they will help you arrive at where you need to be, funding-wise and otherwise. Amy Jo may have a bit of notoriety as the Pink Power Ranger, but that was only one part of getting her campaign over $75,000 in funding. While phase one of the campaign was about catering to the *Power Ranger* subset of her fan base, phase two became all about *The Space Between* itself and immersing her audience in what this film is about, why it's important to her, and most importantly, why they should feel as privileged to help make *The Space Between* happen as Amy Jo felt privileged to invite them to join her on the journey.

Again, when the space between campaigner and crowd is this small, there's no minding the gap — you can just walk right in.

• • •

AT HOME AWAY FROM HOME:
TILT THE TOWN

DURING ITS KICKSTARTER campaign, *Tilt* was first billed as "an independent film collaboration" because it brought together a trio of talented filmmakers to create the "independent thriller" *Tilt* would become after raising $15,606. Julie Keck and Jessica King, the writing and filmmaking duo behind their company King is a Fink Productions, teamed up with filmmaker Phil Holbrook after some conversations on Twitter about possibly working together on a project. The only thing that separated Phil from these two architects of mischief was physical distance — Julie and Jessica hail from Chicago while Phil is situated in the small town of Brainerd, Minnesota. But even that didn't stop them. Julie and Jessica took off to Brainerd to talk about what would ultimately be a successful gathering from which *Tilt* the film and crowdfunding campaign would emerge.

But that's not all that materialized. During the scriptwriting process, Jessica had been thinking of ways to play with the *Tilt* story outside of the movie, seeing as how *transmedia storytelling* — telling a story across multiple platforms — is a smart way to grab hold of an audience and get them invested in the entire story. She devised *Tilt* the Town, and it was later when they were talking about possible perks for the Kickstarter campaign that *Tilt* the Town came up again. That's when they decided to roll with it, not knowing how successful an incentive it would be to make people contribute to *Tilt* the crowdfunding campaign.

WHAT IS *TILT* THE TOWN?

39.1. Tilt *the Town and the folks who "live" there come to life as a Google Map thanks to Julie Keck and Jessica King.*

Tilt the Town is a virtual town created from a map of Phil's hometown of Brainerd. The difference is that this town is populated by characters from the film and mapped by specific landmarks used in the film, such as The Last Turn Saloon and the convenience store where Paul, the main character, buys his groceries. There are also landmarks that are not in the film, like Bump & Grind, a coffee shop/dance studio where retired ballerina Sheri Candler teaches, and Lock-N-Load, Jake Stetler's microbrewery.

And who are Sheri Candler and Jake Stetler? They're just two of 170 Kickstarter backers-turned-*Tilt* the Towners by the writing prowess of King is a Fink. Every backer who contributed $15 to the *Tilt* campaign received a personalized bio about his or her role in *Tilt* the Town. For many crowdfunders, this may have been too much effort to put into one single backer, never mind 170 of them. Even Julie and Jessica admit they had no idea how much work would go into it, or how successful it would ultimately be. But it was this level of personalization that made *Tilt* the Town the successful enterprise it was. There's that, and the fact that Julie and Jessica did so at such a low pledge amount. Most crowdfunders might consider doing something of this magnitude at the $50 or $100 perk level, but not at $15, which just about everyone can afford. Look at the detail of my bio, for instance:

> Backer #21: John Trigonis was the 1st person from his family to graduate from Harvard Law School. Amongst his very brainy friends, he was the very 1st to pass the bar (the 1st time), the 1st to land a fancy job, and the 1st... no, ONLY one to walk out of the courtroom and quit his job after the 1st day of his 1st case.
>
> It's not that John wasn't good at it; it's that he knew he was going to win. John was defending a large fishing conglomerate from Brainerd aquaculturist Roger Hjulstrom's accusation that their practices were unsafe to local species. John knew that he could counter Roger's claims and even stick him with the Fish Inc.'s legal bill, but it just didn't feel like the right thing to do. So he quit.
>
> His adoring parents supported his decision, of course (they love their little Johnny), but they were a little taken aback when John announced that he wanted to move to Brainerd to be the resident puppeteer. However, John thought being a career puppeteer was only logical. He could make up stories, make his puppets fight, and then make them make up at the end, without messy legal entanglements. Happily ever after.
>
> John hosts his puppet shows from an elaborate hand-built stage which he pulls around town on the back of his motorcycle. The stage box is just big enough for him to hide himself in while his puppets tell his stories. The stage box also serves as his home. There he sleeps, usually parked under the Brainerd Water Tower, amongst his puppets. Once in a while

he spends the night at Marinell Montales' new condo, waking her up with breakfast in bed and finger puppet love songs. Sometimes he lunches with Andrew Bichler. Sometimes he just sits and celebrates the day he quit being a lawyer.

Admittedly, this is a fancy bit of story to tell for one backer, but aside from the bios, Julie and Jessica wanted to keep their audience, backers, and followers fully engaged, so they continued writing more stories, involving more and more interactions between backers. For instance, Marinell's my fiancée and Andrew Bichler's a friend and *Cerise* supporter, but I've never met Roger Hjulstrom; yet, in *Tilt* the Town, I'm interacting with him in some virtual way, which can lead to further interaction outside of *Tilt* the Town, in the real world. This not only builds up King is a Fink and Phil Holbrook's following on Twitter and Facebook, but also connects others to those networks, which in the future could lead to other collaborations like *Tilt*. In most instances, Julie and Jessica end each bio with "Learn more about the real Eric here" and link us to a website, blog, or other page where we can get to know our fellow *Tilt* backers.

Tilt the Town is really quite ingenious in that sense. By mentioning a new Kickstarter backer on Twitter using his or her handle and by appending #TiltTheTown to your tweet, you're given a key to an entire town being run by a pair of creative, dedicated, and just plain fun young ladies. Yes, they control the stories that are told; in a perfect world, they would have liked for others to interact with one another without King is a Fink being an intermediary, but it would've been very messy in terms of organization. But this truly dynamic crowdfunding duo did a stellar job at building up a considerable following of people and attracting the attention of other individuals in the indie film world, some of whom Julie and Jessica have recently collaborated with on other projects.

How Successful Was *Tilt* the Town?

Julie shared with me a very interesting fact about *Tilt* the Town: "Many people who originally contributed less than $15 eventually upped their pledges to get in on the fun." That says a lot about the success of *Tilt* the Town, not only because people raised their pledge amounts, but because it wasn't the kind of increase that would break the bank. Even if a person had pledged $10, which grants that person regular updates on *Tilt*'s progress and his or her name in the end credits of the film, for only $5 more he or she would unlock a door into a fun-filled virtual reality.

The advent of *Tilt* the Town and all the stories that Julie and Jessica wove into the fabric of their social network created a sort of *Tilt* the Experience that people would not only want in on, but also would want to know more about. For instance, in a description of the actual characters of *Tilt*, we're introduced to a whole bunch of strange and interesting inhabitants of the town. Then we'll notice something called "Crime Scene #1" and then its mysterious description below: "We know you're curious, but please step back behind the caution tape." It's little things like this, situated snugly between in-depth descriptions of The Last Turn Saloon, the police station, and detailed character narratives, that pique our interest in the progression of the *Tilt* storyline. That, and the fact that we remember the tagline from the invitation video — "Where do you bury your secrets?" — tell us that something's not right in the state of *Tilt* the Town, yet here we are, in one form or another, waiting in anticipation for something to happen.

Five Years Later: Is *Tilt* the Town a Buried Secret?

Tilt the Town is alive and well and living in Brainerd, MN, near Chicago, IL, in Jersey City, NJ, and any- and everywhere there's an Internet connection. Julie and Jessica have succeeded in making their virtual town *our* virtual town, and giving to the indie film and crowdfunding communities something to talk about for years to come. Not only that, they have also put together a PDF "storybook" version of *Tilt* the Town, hyperlinked and complete with the Google Map, all 170 backer bios, locations, and even an index for easily finding specific backers or aspects of *Tilt* the Town that someone may be interested in learning more about, except where the secrets are buried; that's for when we watch the film.

Trignosis #3

• • •

SYNCED UP WITH DETAILS
AND NOSTALGIA

As MENTIONED VERY early on, there is no foolproof way to go about crowdfunding for your indie film, but as long as you have one or two interesting and innovative things going on in your campaign, you'll most likely come out on top. A great example of this is the campaign for the short film *Sync*, which found crowdfunding success on Indiegogo by raising $405 over its initial goal of $3,000 through a masterfully executed campaign spearheaded by Seattle-based filmmaker Brendon Fogle.

REMEMBER WHEN... THE POWER OF NOSTALGIA

Brendon starts out with a standard, personal invitation video. He then goes a step further and shares a question with his potential funders — "Do you remember the first album you ever bought?" — and then a brief story about the first album he ever got and the feeling it gave him to hold a CD in his hand as opposed to downloading music onto an MP3 player. This intro sets the tone of the movie's storyline brilliantly — Sync revolves around a grandfather who's trying to connect with his MP3ed-in grandson through the gift of records. As for incentives, Brendon starts off with one of the more typical ones: stickers. And although they're very cool stickers, they're a ruse, because the architecture of the Sync campaign reveals a "Sweet Spot" of truly exceptional, personalized perks further down the line.

As he was planning out his Indiegogo, Brendon was sure about one thing: He wanted to create a product and campaign that was fun, and he also wanted to offer perks that not only movie fans would enjoy, like movie posters, T-shirts, and producer credits, but also ones that others would enjoy as well. Therefore, holding on tight to the theme of vinyl and the overlaying concept of nostalgia, Brendon offered a piece of himself starting at the $33 perk level by giving funders a record from his very own record collection.

It's a 3-D! incentive like this that can mean the difference between backers settling for a sticker at $12 or upping their contribution so they can receive something truly memorable and even more tangible. That's what did it for me when I became a proud backer of *Sync*, as I mentioned earlier. I wondered just what record I might get, and I was very pleased when I received *Sammy Davis Jr.'s Greatest Hits* in the mail two weeks later, as well as my sticker, of course.

The nostalgia factor doesn't stop at receiving a record from Brendon's own personal collection. At $78, Brendon turns his attention from crowdfunding filmmaker to Photoshop artist,

40.1. Sync's *"Blue Note Treatment"* on one of my own photos magically turns it into a vintage album cover from the 1960s.

turning photos of *Sync*'s mild-mannered funders into super-hip album covers. By giving a photograph what Brendon calls the "Blue Note Treatment," he transforms that old Christmas photo of you into a vintage-looking record from the 1960s. He even did one for me as a test, though I would have happily upped my contribution to be a part of this cool perk (see image 40.1 on the previous page).

THE DESIRE'S IN THE DETAILS

Besides these hip and original perks at the $33 and $78 levels — what Brendon calls the "Sweet Spot" — snuggly placed between the more standard definition incentives of shout-outs and stickers ($3 – $12), T-shirts and producer credits ($128 – $256), what also stands out in Brendon's campaign for *Sync* is his impeccable attention to detail. For instance, each perk has its own nifty title attached to it. "Delicious Vinyl," "33 1/3 RPMazing," and "Bad Mama Gramophone" are neat, fun titles that add a lighthearted feel to Brendon's campaign. Then, when you read the descriptions of the perks, they are not only humorous and airy, but play on the idea of vinyl and records, as in Brendon's $12 perk: "Side A: All of the above. Side B: Plus a digital download of the film, and a *Sync* sticker (perfect for pimping your laptop or Trapper Keeper)."

Also, as you've no doubt already noticed, the perk amounts are not the standard $5 and $50 price points, but instead are based on record RPMs, like 12, 33, and 78. What about the $3 level, which grants funders a spot on *Sync*'s "playlist" and a thank-you in the end credits of the film? That's a play on "MP3." Everything in Brendon's campaign is relevant to the film's content and storyline, making for a more engaging experience from day one to deadline's end.

THE VANCE CONNORS TAPES

Amidst all of Brendon's masterfully crafted campaigning for *Sync*, there comes Vance Connors. Who is Vance Connors, you ask? He's Brendon's alter ego, ace in the hole, and an ingenious way to help drive more traffic to *Sync*'s Indiegogo and keep fresh content flowing on Brendon's Facebook and Twitter pages. Brendon grew up watching late-night infomercials, and thinking back to those nostalgic days, the idea to create his own infomercials dawned on him. It would serve as an interesting, relevant way to explain the perks he was offering and keep the campaign playful and immediate. Thus, Vance Connors was born, taking inspiration from celebrity endorsers like Tony Little, Ron Popeil, and Billy Blanks, who lit up his living room at three in the morning back when there were fewer than 2,000 channels to watch on the television set.

40.2. *Vance Connors* — Sync *spokesperson and all-around hepcat.*

That's Brendon starring as Vance in three videos in which he introduces his $12, $33, and $78 "Sweet Spot" perks. The videos are as vintage as many of the other aspects of *Sync*'s campaign, and include brightly colored backgrounds over which Vance is superimposed, cheesy graphics, and video noise synonymous with

1980s analog technology. The details are what make this campaign a memorable one instead of only a memory.

It's Brendon's attention to the details and commitment to his film and Indiegogo that made *Sync*'s time in the crowdfunding arena as entertaining as it was successful. It's this kind of fine scrutiny that potential contributors want to see, with elements from your film connected all the way through your campaign. Whatever the genre, mood, and tone of your film might be, you should strive to have your campaign reflect each by going the distance and making every dot of your campaign connect to every dot of your film so it all counts for something special and stands the test of time.

• • •

How Do You Direct
[A Gary King Musical] —
Build Your Brand

Chapter Fifty-Four of the *Tao Te Ching* tells us that by cultivating virtue, or *Te*, in oneself, virtue becomes real. At the beginning of *Batman Begins*, Ra's al Ghul tells an angry Bruce Wayne, "If you make yourself more than just a man, if you devote yourself to an ideal, you become something else entirely." Many times through this book I've stated that people give to people, but that is only partially true. People give to people who present themselves as something more than mere men and women because of their devotion to their films, an intense passion for filmmaking, or their own urge to leave a mark on the world. In being this type of person, you are not only a filmmaker or a crowdfunder anymore. You cultivate what author Steven Pressfield refers to as your *personal culture*, and what the rest of the world knows as your *brand*, which can be a powerful tool, when properly used, to achieve your crowdfunding goal and much more.

Gary King ran two successful Kickstarters for his feature-length movie musical *How Do You Write a Joe Schermann Song*. The first pulled in $31,101 for its initial production funds, and the second yielded $18,031 in completion funds, mainly so Gary could record a live orchestra playing the songs featured in the film. At the time, running two campaigns for the same film was seldom done, and not very successful. Now it's fairly commonplace, though success still rests in how one runs these campaigns. Gary is a master at branding and marketing, but beneath it all is a humility that keeps him grounded, and that allows him to present his brand as an extension of himself, because that's exactly what his brand is: himself. Part of this Gary King brand is *innovation*, but Gary's not only innovative in his crowdfunding circles. He's been innovative since the first day he picked up a camera as a kid and decided he wanted to tell stories through the medium of the movies. In the years that followed, he simply amplified this resolve and married his passion for art to the commerce that gets it made. When most filmmakers stray away from the business part of show business, Gary embraces it and, more importantly, uses it for his own gain and the benefit of his audience.

THE FIRST *JOE SCHERMANN* CAMPAIGN

During Gary's first campaign, when crowdfunding was still relatively new, he made sure to follow in the footsteps of contemporary success stories like *Jens Pulver: Driven* and *Cerise*. Gary made a very personal invitation video in which he is simply being himself and casually tells viewers about his idea for his movie musical. He even delves into exactly why he wants to direct a musical more in the vein of *Rent* and *Chicago* than the film *Once*. From his *Flash Gordon* T-shirt to his little cat gazing into the camera, the video gives us information, a sense of Gary's world, and a smile.

Gary also had a lot of help in his initial crowdfunding campaign for *How Do You Write a Joe Schermann Song*. One of the main people by his side from crowdfunding through completion has been his lead actress, Christina Rose. She not only promoted the campaign just as much as Gary did across his social networks, but she also costarred in Gary's campaign video singing songs alongside Joe Schermann, the film's lead actor and songwriter. This also gives us a sense of a tight-knit *connection*, not only between Gary and his actors, but Gary and his backers, which is another selling point in Gary's personal culture. Not every director can get his or her actors to endorse a film with the same gusto, let alone help crowdfund it.

Aside from Gary's invitation for his first Kickstarter, he also put in a lot of time interacting with the indie film community, as well as reaching out proactively to film websites and influential bloggers asking if they might help spread the word about his campaign. And he constantly kept his backers updated every step of the way; Gary posted a total of forty-four updates to all of his 239 contributors. For Gary, *consistency* is key.

But like any campaign, a lull is inevitable, and it was during such a time that Gary and Christina got together and came up with an idea to revitalize the campaign. Members of the *Joe Schermann* cast would sing and perform a song in a video at the request of any backer who pledged $300 or more. "It brought in a lot of money," Gary told me, and it made six backers quite happy. So the innovation didn't stop for a moment through this campaign. As mentioned in Chapter Twenty-Four, a lull can be viewed as simply taking the time necessary to reevaluate the direction of your campaign and make interesting, engaging choices on how to continue it and keep its momentum on the rise.

THE SECOND *JOE SCHERMANN* CAMPAIGN

By the time Gary began his next Kickstarter for the same project, he was seeking the funds needed to hire a sixty-piece orchestra to record all the songs for *How Do You Write a Joe Schermann Song*. By this time, the Internet was much more saturated with crowd-funding campaigns of all kinds. Like any brand name with some new competition encroaching on the market and the possibility of it stealing some of his campaign's shine, Gary changed up his game and did a few things differently this time around.

One of the main things Gary changed was keeping his backers a little less updated than he did in his previous campaign. Compare those forty-four backer updates in his first to the mere ten in the next. Gary's rationale was that since it is essentially the same campaign, he didn't want to add to the already intense campaign saturation by constantly promoting and giving backer updates on a daily or weekly basis. Instead, he kept his backers informed only about significant news regarding the progress of the campaign. Gary also continued with some tactics that worked in his prior campaign and modified others, evidenced in a "Reward Update" Gary posted, which announced that his team was compiling a list of words that Joe Schermann would incorporate into a song to be performed by members of the cast.

An interesting choice Gary made was deciding to keep his rewards the same as they were in his original campaign one year before this one was launched, the idea being that the incentives would still be relevant to new backers just joining the *Joe Schermann* campaign. For prior backers, as Gary mentions in his campaign video, their current pledge amount would be added to their previous pledge amount so they could qualify for a higher reward, which was a pretty risky tactic, but one that seemed to work out just fine with a whopping 244 backers pledging to this second campaign.

Keeping with the theme of personalization from the original campaign, Gary's invitation is just as personal, and this time includes lead actress Christina Rose seated beside him on a couch talking to the viewer with Gary. One aspect of this video that struck me as truly brilliant is Gary demonstrating what the music would sound like if it were recorded with a full sixty-piece orchestra versus only a small assortment of instruments, and that was one of his strongest selling points. That's one of the reasons I jumped on board — the orchestration sounded excellent, and I wanted Gary to have a chance to get that kind of sound for his movie.

According to Gary, the first campaign was about outreach by spreading the word about the *Joe Schermann* Kickstarter campaign to a wide array of individuals who might help bring in the funds needed to make the film. The focus of his second campaign shifted

41.1. *"The Pose" that helped Gary King launch over two thousand likes between his three most well-known films.*

from getting in touch with bloggers and film websites and constant interactions to making the campaign more interactive for prior and potential backers alike. Because of the aforementioned "overcrowding" of campaigns streaming past our Twitter and Facebook feeds, it may not have been enough for Gary, Christina, and the indie film community to tweet and retweet the same tweets just to have them get lost in a flood of countless others. Like any brand worth believing in, you have to stand out.

Minimal Risk = Minimal Reward

Perhaps one of the most interesting things about Gary and his two campaigns for *How Do You Write a Joe Schermann Song* is the fact that never once was he afraid to take a risk or try something new, something that no one else had attempted. Much the way it is in filmmaking, so it goes with crowdfunding. There are risks involved, especially when you choose Kickstarter over Indiegogo or go for fixed over flexible funding with Indiegogo. But as a crowdfunder, you simply can't afford to think of the risks. You have got to take them, but in a smart way, like Gary did. You have to be innovative, personable, and unwavering in your desire to get your film fully funded.

BELIEF IS AN ADDICTION

In a post called "Lessons Learned in the Land of Crowdfunding," which Gary wrote for his blog An Indie Life, Gary outlines all the important takeaways he received after his first campaign, which he then incorporated into his second. One of those most important ones is to "believe in yourself and your project." That's how you not only build a product like *How Do You Write a Joe Schermann Song*, *What's Up Lovely*, or *New York Lately*, two prior films written, directed, and self-financed by the Los Angeles–based filmmaker, but how you build a brand like Gary King: You have to show you care not only about this one product, but every aspect of it, from the writing to the cast and crew, all the way down to the audience itself.

Therefore, when we see a likeable, charismatic person like Gary and we listen to what he or she has to say, that person may become even more captivating because of the things he or she says or believes in. These kinds of people bring out the best in us. Sometimes we admire them for their passion and drive, and that builds not only respect, but also a following. We root for these people. It almost doesn't matter whether we like the final products because we appreciate the fact that the creators followed their dreams from starting gun to finish line and now have something to show for all that time and effort spent crowdfunding, writing, shooting, and editing.

That's how you build [a Gary King musical]. That's how you build a brand of jeans that anyone would want to wear.

Trignosis #5

• • •

A "Celebrity Campaign" *Miles Ahead* of the Rest

I KNOW WHAT you're thinking: *John, didn't you mention back in Chapter Thirty-Four that you weren't going to talk about celebrity campaigns in this edition?* Yes, I did mention that, didn't I?

Ever since *Veronica Mars* became the first campaign in the film and video category to raise over $1M in crowdfunding, celebrity crowd-funding campaigns have become more and more commonplace. We've witnessed a couple beloved television shows get a renaissance, a cult stoner comedy get a sequel fan-funded and the captain and pilot of the *Serenity* get behind the controls of a very successful web series, and the latest Spike Lee joint get green-lit, all thanks to crowds that wanted to see these film and video projects get made.

There are a few reasons to take a look at the Indiegogo for *Miles Ahead*, a film about jazz artist Miles Davis, directed by and starring Don Cheadle. The main reason is that it's really the first celebrity campaign to raise a substantial amount in funding — $344,582 between deadline and InDemand funding — that did not receive any negative sentiments from the press or the public, which I frequently refer to as "Brafflash." It was Zach Braff's Kickstarter for *Wish I Was Here* that got raked over the coals for a variety of reasons ranging from Braff's acceptance of gap financing for the film from Worldview Entertainment after stating that he thinks it would be in bad taste to take industry money to Kickstarter backers getting snubbed for a thank-you and many of them not being admitted into the Sundance premiere, many of whom paid premium dollars to get into.

Since the *Wish I Was Here* campaign, plenty of celebrities have received similar criticism, which has sparked discussion on the integrity of celebrities using crowdfunding to finance their own independent films, be it Spike Lee's solipsistic first campaign video to Melissa Joan Hart's canceling her Kickstarter before it had a chance to end at 2% funded on its $2M goal. It's not that there's necessarily a different way for a well-known personality to crowd-fund his or her film. It's actually quite the opposite: The celebrity needs to go about crowdfunding just like any other truly independent filmmaker would, and that means being creative, open, and allowing their fans ultimate access, which many of these celebrities are not willing to do as freely as one might expect.

Looking at the other side of the coin, however, *Miles Ahead* is a celebrity campaign, and the only difference is in volume, not only of funds raised, but of how many fans one has who can help raise that funding. Even a celebrity campaign requires proper strategy, and that's where Don and his team excelled with everything including up-close-and-personal access, strategic sponsorships, and utilizing another celebrity friend's network to help drive contributions to make *Miles Ahead* a very successful Indiegogo, and one that escaped any kind of Brafflash by its conclusion.

THERE AIN'T NO NATION LIKE "GOGO NATION"

Having worked directly with the team behind the *Miles Ahead* Indiegogo, one of the first things I remember saying to them was that we need as much access to Don as possible. That meant we'd need to see him in the invitation video and in other videos, too, as well as through not only higher-end incentives, but mid-tier and low-level perks as well. Of course, I got a little bit of pushback on just how much access they'd be able to get. Then I mentioned that in order to escape any kind of backlash Don might incur, we needed to bring him down to the level of the people he'd be seeking funding from: the crowd.

What made this easier was that Don had an amazing story to tell. It was a personal one, but it wasn't just about how a movie about Miles Davis *needed* to be made that wasn't your typical biopic, but a deeper exploration into the tortured life of this pioneer of modern jazz. That's the story of the film, and as we learned in Chapter Thirty-Four, we need *two stories*. The other story was Don's own, and how he had originally tried to pitch the film for many years to studios, but it kept on getting rejected. Why? Because Don was attaching himself as the film's director, and since he had never directed a film before, it proved a difficult sell. (Yes, even for someone like Don Cheadle.) So he was going to the crowd not only to finance a film about Miles Davis, but also to assure his directorial debut.

Don recorded an amazing campaign video, which featured him speaking directly to his potential contributors and practicing his trumpet for the role that will define Miles Davis for generations to come. And he didn't stop there. Through the course of the Indiegogo, Don and the *Miles Ahead* team kept their backers — the "Gogo Nation," as Don christened them in his first video update just a few days after the campaign had begun — in the loop of all things *Miles Ahead*–related, offering stills from the set, a pic of him before throwing the first pitch at a Cincinnati Reds game while he was there shooting the film, and testimonial videos from jazz legends all over the country.

To this day, Don and his team still keep the Gogo Nation updated on all things *Miles Ahead*, from festival screenings to being selected as the closing night film at the New York Film Festival to being picked up for distribution by Sony Pictures Classics. Don truly is a face in his crowd.

3-D! INCENTIVES FOR DAYS — NO IMAX REQUIRED

With a campaign like this, you simply can't skimp on the incentives. The people know you have access to things that they most likely do not, so you need to offer that access. When a nonprofit organization runs a large-scale event with celebrity endorsements, and, say, Leonardo DiCaprio offers a private dinner on his yacht for a contribution of $100,000 to the cause, people may love the cause, but they're really paying for the access to the celebrity who's supporting it with his or her time, signed items, or other incentives.

That said, *Miles Ahead* played to the Gogo Nation very well by way of its Indiegogo perks. Because Don is very close to members of the Davis family, he had access to the Miles Davis Estate, so some of the higher-end incentives during the campaign were limited-edition pieces of Miles' artwork, vintage posters, and even a trumpet case filled with Miles' entire collection of music and other memorabilia.

It didn't stop there, though. Many of these items were priced at the $1,250 level and higher; the trumpet case, limited to three, sold one at $1,500. There was more standard-definition merchandise, as one would expect: T-shirts and hoodies, both standard and rare, CD collections, iPhone cases, and even hard copies of *Miles Davis: The Collected Artwork*; and at the $12,000 and up levels were the usual suspects of associate producer credits and set visits, with lots of previous perks included in those packages. Lots of value if you could afford it, of course.

Thrown into the mix, however, were a bunch of Don-centric perks. At $8,500, a contributor could play a round of golf with Don; for a contribution of $7,500, backers could have lunch with him; for $1,000, they would get a T-shirt, hoodie, and thanks in the credits of the film, plus Don would say a personal thank-you in a YouTube video. Still a tad pricey? Well, how about a five-minute Skype call with Don for $100, or an Instagram shout-out from Don at the low price of $45? There were only five and twenty available, respectively, and they all sold out very quickly.

In celebrity crowdfunding for indie film, access is everything. And Don gave his fans the most value possible, even at lesser amounts of money.

Harmonies in Partnership

Partnerships are also an important facet in crowdfunding of this kind. There's a lot that goes on behind the scenes of a campaign as well wrought and run as the *Miles Ahead* Indiegogo. One of the first tasks is finding out what kinds of partnerships you can work out between individuals and organizations for incentives, promotional opportunities, or both. Don got many of his influential friends to tweet the campaign to their followings and post updates on their Facebook pages about *Miles Ahead*. He was also able to secure back-stage passes to a Robert Glasper and even a Nas concert, which sold immediately once they were announced on social media for $1,000 and $2,000, respectively. The *Miles Ahead* team also worked with SONOS, the popular music streaming service and speakers that enable you to stream your music in multiple rooms of your house or apartment, to cross-promote the campaign.

Again, crowdfunding an independent feature film when you've got some level of celebrity attached to your name depends less on reputation, reputation, reputation and more on access, access, and even more access. The thing that most celebrity campaigners like Braff, Hart, and even Spike do wrong is keep themselves standing atop the pedestal that their fans have set them on in the first place. Crowdfunding requires stepping down from that pedestal tempo-rarily and becoming a part of that crowd, and that means offering more value for less money, so that everyone is treated the same, from the $50 contributor to the $15,000 one. Otherwise, that same crowd that put you up on that pedestal will pull you right off, and then all you're left with are the funds, and that's only half the reward and privilege of crowdfunding.

Conclusion

• • •

THE *YOU* OF CROWDFUNDING

It's HARD WORK making a movie. It's harder work securing the funding to make one. And even though crowdfunding has afforded many creatives the most accessible bridge connecting first draft to finished product, it's still hard work to architect and maintain an engaging and appealing campaign. The good news is that, as film-makers, in particular, we don't have to be Kevin Smith or the next Ed Burns to acquire the funding we need to turn our script pages into screen frames.

The ways we crowdfund will undoubtedly change in the years to come, especially in light of United States legislation like the JOBS Act. Laws like this can dramatically shift the landscape of crowdfunding for better or worse. Successful crowdfunding is no exact science and may forever exist in a perpetual state of trial and error. It's only because of past victories that we know as much as we do about what works best and what can be detrimental for a film campaign. As Indiegogo's Head Film Campaign Strategist, I've worked with some of the top crowdfunded indie films around, and I've seen firsthand what methods still work wonders for and which tactics have lost their flair for bringing in the funds. This is why *Crowdfunding for Filmmakers — 2nd Edition* is full of even more specific examples from projects that have found success by trying, possibly failing, then trying something different, and repeating the cycle all over again in the next crowdfunding campaign.

One important truth to keep in mind is that raising funds online for your film is very similar to tweeting about a screening of your recent short at a local festival or getting people to like your movie on Facebook. At the end of the day, the *Tao* of crowdfunding is the "Way" of publicity, and today, "publicity" really means being a person before you petition, or saying hello before asking for funding. Even the world's leading companies have turned toward social networking for maximum outreach, but you don't have to be a Taoist master to see they're going about it more socially than traditional advertising dictates. There's now a face behind most companies, someone who's extending a virtual hand to embrace yours in a Digital Age handshake that will welcome you further into the fold of his or her product. That's what crowdfunding your indie film needs to be like, too, but it seldom starts with the Do-It-Yourself filmmaker, the 24fps dreamer, or the aspiring movie actor. It usually begins with the *real* you.

It's quite easy to disregard this fact, and if you do, don't panic — it doesn't necessarily mean you won't reach your crowdfunding goal. But remember this: Crowdfunding is not only about raising funds, but also about building your audience for this film and your future projects. Therefore, we should let go of all the misconceptions about film financing — how it's supposed to be secured by suit-and-tie producers and investors with no care for your film's artistic integrity, or paid for out-of-pocket — and instead accept the fact that *we* are the ones now responsible for acquiring that funding. As filmmakers, we are not only artists, but entrepreneurs (or *artrepreneurs*, as I like to refer to us) too, and we would do well to keep these two fundamental forces in balance at all times.

The tools for crowdfunding your next short or feature-length film, web series, or video project are all here in this book — from choosing the right platform to expertly navigating the social media spectrum. No matter what technological innovations or legislative measures evolve to further enhance online fundraising, the essence of successful crowdfunding will remain firmly rooted in the soil of personalization, and the heart of your campaign will always lie with you.

ADDITIONAL RESOURCES FOR CROWDFUNDING FILMMAKERS

THE SECOND EDITION of *Crowdfunding for Filmmakers* will no doubt prove an invaluable asset to help get you through a crowdfunding campaign, whether it's your first time fundraising online or you're a seasoned crowdfunder in need of a refresher course. It's always a good idea to keep up to date with the future of crowdfunding. Stay in the know about which new campaigns are making waves across the indie film community and examine how those film-makers are achieving both innovation and success. But this in itself can be quite laborious.

Luckily, most filmmakers who finish a crowdfunding campaign usually take some time to write a brief blog post that explores what they've learned from their campaigning, what they would've done differently, what definitely worked, and, more times than not, how they never thought crowdfunding would require as much time and effort as it does. It's in your best interest to keep a keen eye on film campaigns for films like yours and be sure to read those insightful afterthoughts about crowdfunding.

I always recommend starting at the source: your crowdfunding platform of choice.

ON-PLATFORM EDUCATION

Since every crowdfunding platform has its own language and suggested strategies for running a successful campaign, I always recommend reading the platform's educational materials first, be it a downloadable handbook or information in their help centers or from their blogs. I've examined a bunch of them, and I highly recommend subscribing to the Indiegogo Blog as your primary resource for any kind of how-to information on crowdfunding. (Full disclosure: As I mentioned earlier, I do work for Indiegogo as the company's Head Film Campaign Strategist, and I frequently provide content strictly for filmmakers on the blog.) A second worthwhile blog can be found on the film-only platform Seed & Spark at *https://www.seedandspark.com/blog*. There are so many informative articles, from how to build your audiences before launch to pieces about what technology you as a crowdfunding filmmaker should be using for your next campaign.

Indiegogo and Kickstarter both have their own free resources for how to run a successful campaign. Indiegogo, however, has an actual Film Handbook, which was written by the Indiegogo Film Team and me, and provides a sturdy foundation for any filmmaker, indie or otherwise, to run a stellar campaign.

And lastly, there's RocketHub's Crowdfunding Success School, located on the website's blog at *https://www.rockethub.com/educa-tion*. The Success School was created by RocketHub CEO Brian Meece and serves to instruct crowdfunders of all kinds in the basics of online fundraising by focusing on four main phases for success: mastering the basics, preparing to launch, running a live project, and managing funders. Although the Success School is not film-centric, it covers all one needs to know in order to run a successful campaign for anything, creative or otherwise.

OTHER FREE RESOURCES FROM THE FIELD

As I mention many times throughout this book, crowdfunding is all about community, so it's no wonder that most filmmakers upon conclusion of their campaigns, and after they get a few hours of much-deserved rest, will usually pen a blog post about their experiences. What follows is a list of such pieces that I recommend each and every one of you read before you even think of crowdfunding an indie film.

To make it easier, a good friend of mine named Bella Wonder, who runs a blog site called Wonderland, has compiled a very comprehensive list of blog posts from fellow filmmakers who've launched successful and not-so-successful crowdfunding campaigns. It's been aptly named "The Crowdfunder's Bible," and includes my original "Tao of Crowdfunding" blog post "Three Ps for a Successful Film Campaign." It also features many bits of insight from crowdfunders mentioned throughout this book like Jeanie Finlay (*Sound It Out*), Meg Pinsonneault (*Gwapa (Beautiful)*), and Gary King (*How Do You Write a Joe Schermann Song*). It also pulls examples from lots of others who've seen crowdfunding success, such as Oklahoma Ward, who raised $10,352 of his $10,000 Kickstarter goal for a documentary on the making of two hardcore indie horror films, *Crawl or Die* (directed by Ward) and *Screen* (directed by David Paul Baker) and David Branin, who raised $16,203 of a $15,000 goal on Kickstarter for his feature-length film *Goodbye Promise*.

You can find Bella's "Crowdfunder's Bible" here: *http://bellawonder.com/the-crowdfunders-bible/*

Perhaps the best article I've ever read on crowdfunding an independent film has to be "The Story of a Crowdfunding Campaign — *Iron Sky: The Coming Race*" by Timo Vuorensola. This rather lengthy, but insightful piece will prove to be one of your best allies in the journey that is crowdfunding an indie film. Filled with graphs, some data, and the "Holy Trinity" of unique perks, good content, and constant updating, which helped Timo and his team raise over $560,000 during their second campaign for *Iron Sky: The Coming Race*, this piece will prove that with hard work comes the spoils of a well-wrought film campaign.

44.1. *After putting it to practice, the filmmakers behind* Iron Sky: The Coming Race *introduced the world to "The Holy Trinity."*

You can find "The Story of a Crowdfunding Campaign – *Iron Sky: The Coming Race*" here: *http://www.ironsky.net/blog/ the-story-of-a-crowdfunding-campaign-iron-sky-the-coming-race/*

Lastly, here is a list of a handful of other blog posts, articles, and stories — some of which have been mentioned in this book — that I think will also offer much insight and helpful tips to lead you to a crowdfunding victory:

- "The Etiquette of Crowdfunding: A Recipient's View" by Pete Brook (Prison Photography): *http://prisonphotography.wordpress. com/2012/01/21/the-etiquette-of-crowdfunding-a-recipients-view/*

- "The Newbie's Guide to Social Networking" by Meg Pinson-neault (Film Courage): *http://filmcourage.com/node/833*

- "5 Sobering Realities of Crowd-Funding" by Princeton Holt (Film Courage): *http://filmcourage.com/index.php?q=content/5-sobering-realities-crowd-funding*

- "5 Ways You Are Using Twitter Incorrectly to Promote Your Film's Crowdfunding Campaign" by Richard "RB" Botto (Medium): *https://medium.com/@Stage32online/5-ways-you-are-using-twitter-incorrectly-to-promote-your-films-crowdfunding-campaign-246e4a84c137*

- "10 Social Media Tips for a Successful Crowdfunding Campaign" by Julie Keck (Media Shift): *http://mediashift.org/2013/12/10-things-to-know-about-social-media-savvy-crowd-funding/*

A COUPLE OF OTHER BOOKS WORTH THE MONEY

Aside from the free resources above, I also recommend that every filmmaker and content creator pick up a copy of the following books in print or for their tablets, which get deep into the trenches of how to use social media properly:

- *Social Media Charm School: A Guide for Filmmakers & Screenwriters* by Jessica King and Julie Keck: *http://www.amazon.com/Social-Media-Charm-School-Screenwriters-ebook/dp/B00LK5UD10*

- *Jab, Jab, Jab, Right Hook: How to Tell Your Story in a Noisy Social World* by Gary Vaynerchuk: *http://www.amazon.com/Jab-Right-Hook-Story-Social/dp/006227306X/ref=tmm_hrd_swatch_0?_encoding=UTF8&qid=1441164050&sr=1-1*

BIBLIOGRAPHY

Fractured Atlas. "Fiscal Sponsorship: About Fiscal Sponsorship." *http://www.fracturedatlas.org/site/fiscal/*

Holt, Princeton. "5 Sobering Realties of Crowdfunding." *Film Courage.* Last modified November 14, 2011. *http://filmcourage.com/content/5-sobering-realities-crowd-funding*

Margolis, Michael. *Believe Me: Why Your Vision, Brand and Leadership Need a Bigger Story.* New York; Get Storied Press, 2009. PDF edition.

Pierce, Esq., David Albert. "Cinema Law: Why Filmmakers Should be Very, Very Careful About Equity Crowdfunding." *MovieMaker.* Last modified January 6, 2016. *http://www.moviemaker.com/archives/blogs/cinema_law/be-very-very-careful-about-equity-crowdfunding/*

Roderick, Mark. "A Regulation A+ Primer." Flaster/Greenberg, 2015. PDF edition. *http://media.wix.com/ugd/a6407f_049c8c3d7ba 148f9a635fdda6894a763.pdf*

Ryan, Paul F. "A Film in the Crowd." *MovieMaker.* Last modified April 15, 2011. *http://www.moviemaker.com/archives/moviemaking/directing/articles-directing/crowdfunding-kickstarter-indiegogocase-studies-20110427/*

Smith, Nigel. "Jennifer Fox Raises $150,000 for 'My Reincarnation' on Kickstarter." *Indiewire.* Last modified May 31, 2011. *http://www.indiewire.com/article/spiritual_doc_my_reincarnation_bomes_top_raising_finished_film_on_kickstart#*

Tsu, Lao. *Tao Te Ching.* Translated by Gia-Fu Feng and Jane English. New York: Vintage Books, 1989.

Tzu, Sun. *The Art of War.* Translated by Lionel Giles. El Paso: El Paso Norte Press, 2005.

Vaynerchuk, Gary. *Jab, Jab, Jab, Right Hook*. New York: HarperCollins, 2013.

Vuorensola, Timo. "The Story of a Crowdfunding Campaign — Iron Sky: The Coming Race." *Iron Sky*. Last Modified: January 7, 2015. *http://www.ironsky.net/blog/the-story-of-a-crowdfunding-campaign-iron-sky-the-coming-race/*

ABOUT THE AUTHOR

WRITER, INDEPENDENT FILMMAKER, TED speaker, and renowned crowdfunding expert John T. Trigonis has mentored thousands of filmmakers, storymakers, and other creators worldwide to help them craft compelling crowdfunding campaigns that not only reach, but oftentimes exceed, their online fundraising goals.

Through a well-wrought campaign for a short film of his own called *Cerise*, Trigonis put to practice his "Three Ps of Crowdfunding" (now his "Three Ways to Get Your Crowd Into Funding Your Indie Film") and surpassed his fundraising goal, then enticed his crowd again independent of a platform to raise thousands more to submit *Cerise* to film festivals.

After spending a few years as a private crowdfunding consultant for a number of creative campaigns on various platforms, Trigonis was invited aboard Indiegogo's Film Team as its Head Film Campaign Strategist. He works behind the scenes on all of the most successful film and video campaigns like *Super Troopers 2*, *Con Man*, *Iron Sky: The Coming Race*, *Miles Ahead*, *Life Itself*, *Dragon's Lair*, and countless other top-dollar film campaigns, all while continuing to nurture his own creative multimedia projects.

You can contact Trigonis through his website/blog at *http://johntrigonis.com* and/or follow him on Twitter (@Trigonis).

THE WRITER'S JOURNEY
3RD EDITION

MYTHIC STRUCTURE FOR WRITERS

CHRISTOPHER VOGLER

BEST SELLER
OVER 170,000 COPIES SOLD!

See why this book has become an international best seller and a true classic. *The Writer's Journey* explores the powerful relationship between mythology and storytelling in a clear, concise style that's made it required reading for movie executives, screenwriters, playwrights, scholars, and fans of pop culture all over the world.

Both fiction and nonfiction writers will discover a set of useful myth-inspired storytelling paradigms (i.e., "The Hero's Journey") and step-by-step guidelines to plot and character development. Based on the work of Joseph Campbell, *The Writer's Journey* is a must for all writers interested in further developing their craft.

The updated and revised third edition provides new insights and observations from Vogler's ongoing work on mythology's influence on stories, movies, and man himself.

"This book is like having the smartest person in the story meeting come home with you and whisper what to do in your ear as you write a screenplay. Insight for insight, step for step, Chris Vogler takes us through the process of connecting theme to story and making a script come alive."
> – Lynda Obst, Producer, *Sleepless in Seattle, How to Lose a Guy in 10 Days;*
> Author, *Hello, He Lied*

"This is a book about the stories we write, and perhaps more importantly, the stories we live. It is the most influential work I have yet encountered on the art, nature, and the very purpose of storytelling."
> – Bruce Joel Rubin, Screenwriter, *Stuart Little 2, Deep Impact,*
> *Ghost, Jacob's Ladder*

CHRISTOPHER VOGLER is a veteran story consultant for major Hollywood film companies and a respected teacher of filmmakers and writers around the globe. He has influenced the stories of movies from *The Lion King* to *Fight Club* to *The Thin Red Line* and most recently wrote the first installment of *Ravenskull*, a Japanese-style manga or graphic novel. He is the executive producer of the feature film *P.S. Your Cat is Dead* and writer of the animated feature *Jester Till*.

$27.95 · 300 PAGES · ORDER NUMBER 76RLS · ISBN: 193290736x

{ THE MYTH OF MWP }

In a dark time, a light bringer came along, leading the curious and the frustrated to clarity and empowerment. It took the well-guarded secrets out of the hands of the few and made them available to all. It spread a spirit of openness and creative freedom, and built a storehouse of knowledge dedicated to the betterment of the arts.

The essence of the Michael Wiese Productions (MWP) is empowering people who have the burning desire to express themselves creatively. We help them realize their dreams by putting the tools in their hands. We demystify the sometimes secretive worlds of screenwriting, directing, acting, producing, film financing, and other media crafts.

By doing so, we hope to bring forth a realization of 'conscious media' which we define as being positively charged, emphasizing hope and affirming positive values like trust, cooperation, self-empowerment, freedom, and love. Grounded in the deep roots of myth, it aims to be healing both for those who make the art and those who encounter it. It hopes to be transformative for people, opening doors to new possibilities and pulling back veils to reveal hidden worlds.

MWP has built a storehouse of knowledge unequaled in the world, for no other publisher has so many titles on the media arts. Please visit www.mwp.com where you will find many free resources and a 25% discount on our books. Sign up and become part of the wider creative community!

Onward and upward,

Michael Wiese
Publisher/Filmmaker